ON THE MOVE AGAIN?

WHAT WORKS IN CREATING STABILITY FOR LOOKED AFTER CHILDREN

SONIA JACKSON

and

NIGEL THOMAS

Barnardos

First published in 1999 by Barnardo's

Tanners Lane
Barkingside
Ilford
Essex
IG6 1QG

Charity registration no. 216250

A catalogue record for this book is available from the British Library.

ISBN 0 902046 55 1

CONTENTS

ACKNOWLEDGEMENTS

We would like to thank all the people who generously gave us help and advice at various stages in writing this paper. Hugh Mackintosh and Diana McNeish identified stability as a major issue for looked after children and provided much valued support throughout the production of the report. Mike Stein supplied a launch pad and made many useful suggestions, as did Jane Aldgate, Celia Atherton, David Berridge, Celia Beckett, Carol Douglas, Colette McAuley; and from the United States Anthony Maluccio, Edith Fein and Rosalind Folman. We are also grateful to Jerry Roberts, Brian and Kate Cairns, and John Brown for helpful conversations and for access to unpublished material. Thanks also to James Dougan, Steve Harwood, Dr Jarvis and Anne van Meeuwen.

FOREWORD

Most people agree that a cornerstone of good parenting is to provide children with a safe, secure and stable environment in which to grow and develop. Parents strive to provide this for their own children and, thankfully, the majority succeed. For those children who can't experience stability with their own families, the alternative is often parenting by the State. Around 51,000 children and young people are currently looked after by local authorities in England. The figure for looked after children and young people in Scotland is about 12,000, and both Wales and Northern Ireland each have more than 2000 looked after children and young people. Sadly, for many of these children the State is likely to be an erratic parent. Experience has shown that some of the State's children are looked after very well: they flourish and go on to lead successful and fulfilling lives. Others are mistreated or disregarded, many of them thrust into a premature adulthood to carry alone the consequences of the State's neglect.

Concerns about the care of looked after children are not new. Successive research studies, inspection reports and inquiries have highlighted the inconsistencies in policy, practice and planning which are frequently reflected in poor outcomes experienced by children leaving the care system. Among these concerns is the recurring worry about the number of times some children move between placements and the consequences of these moves for their social, educational and emotional development. As the authors of this publication point out, although it is the abuse of children in care that has attracted much attention, it is arguable that instability causes an equal amount of harm to looked after children. There has been a widespread awareness of the damaging effects of instability for many years, yet there is little evidence that matters have improved.

In 1996, Barnardo's Director of Children's Services in Scotland, Hugh Mackintosh and a Barnardo's researcher, Mike Hughes, initiated a monitoring exercise of the moves of 145 children and young people involved with seven Scottish Barnardo's projects. 82 of these young people had already experienced three or more moves before their involvement with Barnardo's. One child of primary age had moved forty times. Children and young people had had up to eleven education placements before coming to the Barnardo's projects.

It was this information which provided the initial impetus for this report. Barnardo's, in common with all other agencies involved in the care of children, have long been aware of the importance of stability for children. Yet, the importance given to stability in theory is frequently not matched in practice. It is not easy to create stability for looked after children whose lives have already been disrupted. Barnardo's aim in commissioning this report was not to suggest that there are simple solutions. Our aims were to explore what research can tell us about the factors that contribute to stability; to make a contribution to developing better planning for children; and to highlight, once more, the importance of doing all in our power to create a stable childhood for some of the most disadvantaged children in Britain.

This report reviews the research evidence which highlights the importance of stability for looked after children, how stability relates to other aspects of quality of care, the factors that help to create stability and what can be done to promote stability in the future.

This report is one of a series of publications produced by Barnardo's as part of a commitment to promoting effective practice with children and young people. The authors, Professor Sonia Jackson and Nigel Thomas are well known for their contributions to research and practice in child welfare, particularly for looked after children. Barnardo's is grateful to both for this valuable contribution to the *What Works?* series.

The *What Works?* series is founded on the belief that children and young people are entitled to services which are based on the best available evidence of effectiveness. Such evidence is not always readily available. As the authors point out in their introduction, there is compelling evidence from research of the damaging effects on children of instability, but it is less clear what can be done to avoid it. Research cannot give us any certainties but it can help to give us direction.

Barnardo's welcomes recent Government initiatives to improve the quality of care for looked after children and the targets set out in Quality Protects to reduce the number of placement moves. However, we believe that more still needs to be done promote stability. In particular, we believe that:

● any decision about a child's placement should seek continuity, with stability of placement being the default option unless there are compelling reasons to seek an alternative;

- more attention should be paid to the ways in which policies and organisational systems and processes undermine stability – all too often the child's behaviour is cited as the cause of a move when the real reasons lie elsewhere;

- more value should be placed on education as a source of continuity in children's lives;

- more attention should be paid to the views of children and young people themselves when planning for their care.

Looking after any child is an important and challenging responsibility. When care is being provided by the State it usually means that things have already gone wrong in that child's life. This places an even greater responsibility on us all to provide the best care possible. Stability is an integral part of good childhood experience. Barnardo's believes that more can be done both to reduce instability in the care system and to minimise the damaging effects when placement changes are unavoidable. This report highlights some of the key messages for policy, practice and management. We hope that these messages will provide some direction to those trying to promote stability and ultimately contribute to better outcomes for looked after children.

Maggie Smith
Director of Children's Services
Barnardo's

CHAPTER I : INTRODUCTION

It is arguable that although sexual abuse attracts far more attention, instability is the source of just as much harm to children who need to be looked after away from home. Coming often from chaotic backgrounds, too many enter a system which inflicts still further damage on their social, emotional and cognitive development by its failure to provide a place where they can be confident of staying for any length of time, and which then labels them as disturbed and disruptive.

We were very pleased to be asked by Barnardo's to undertake this review of the evidence on what works in creating stability for looked after children because our subjective impression as researchers, teachers and participants in policy discussions is that the whole care system has become chronically unstable. It is the exception, as we show in Chapter 4, for a looked after child to stay in one place for any length of time, and many children and young people move repeatedly within a short period.

We need to understand the factors that have contributed to this instability if we are to find ways of overcoming the problem. This is difficult because of the lack of any reliable baseline. Finding direct evidence of what creates stability has proved even more difficult. We had hoped, on beginning this task, that a simple literature review would turn up a mass of studies which we could then evaluate for the quality of their research. To our surprise we found that very little has been published directly on the subject of stability. Stability is not the same as permanency, on which there is a large American literature. This is almost entirely concerned with family preservation and/or reunification, and to a lesser extent, in the case of long-term foster care or adoption, with the continuation or disruption of the *first* placement. Very few studies take much interest in what happens to the child after that, or indeed in the child's experience at all.

As David Quinton and his colleagues (1997) have pointed out, there are several stages in research on any topic. First the subject has to be recognised as a matter for concern, then a number of possible remedies are tried and some emerge as received best practice. This stage is usually followed by several small-scale descriptive studies, often coming out of practice, and arguing the case for change. There may then be research using larger and more systematically recruited samples, at which point the assumptions behind the practice can be formulated into research questions and testable hypotheses. There is little doubt that in the case of stability we are only at the first stage.

At the start of this work we wrote to fourteen leading child welfare researchers in Britain and America asking them to nominate the two or three most important pieces of research bearing on the question of stability for children in out-of-home care. We are most grateful to those who replied, but few could think of anything to recommend, and many of the publications that were suggested were tangential to the subject. Our initial idea of identifying a relatively small number of up-to-date research studies using high quality research methodology turned out to be unrealistic. We have instead provided an overview, highlighting research which seems particularly relevant to the question of stability, though this is rarely its main focus, and directing attention to findings which have been replicated.

Apart from research, we planned to identify and describe schemes or projects designed to enhance stability for children in public care. To this end we used all our personal contacts and also wrote letters for publication in *Community Care* and *Professional Social Work* asking anyone who knew of such schemes to contact us. We received many expressions of interest but few positive suggestions. We followed these up and have included some of them in Chapter 7. They are mostly in the early second stage of Quinton's timetable, having been in operation for variable amounts of time, and only one, the Kent Family Placement Scheme, which evolved into the Pro-Teen agency, has been formally evaluated.

It is the norm in the United States for evaluation to be built into all funded projects, and although the quality of the evaluation is often variable, it does usually ensure proper record-keeping and some means of assessing outcomes. This is far from true in Britain, and in some cases, in the absence of any published material, we were only able to make any comment on the effectiveness of the scheme or project by analysing the raw data ourselves, though this was not part of our brief.

People who have to make hard decisions about how children should be looked after when they cannot live with their families often find research reports irritating because they so seldom come down on one side or the other, hedging their conclusions with cautious reservations. The truth is that research is about generalisations but practice is about individuals. We are very clear that stability matters enormously to separated children and should be given far higher priority in all decisions that are made about and with them. On the other hand it is not the *only* thing that matters, and we would be sorry if the emphasis which we necessarily give it in this report were to lead to practitioners resisting a change of placement that would be in the child's interest or which the child him or herself strongly desires.

The research evidence is compelling that instability and many changes of placement are extremely damaging to children, but less clear on what can be done to avoid it. It will never be possible to achieve stability in the sense of one single alternative or permanent placement for every child in public care, but by applying the knowledge we have, and the resources that are necessary, we believe it is possible greatly to reduce movement within the care system. The research is not good enough to say for certain 'What Works in Creating Stability' but we can certainly suggest 'what helps'. There is much that can be done to minimise the painful effects of placement changes when they are unavoidable, and by emphasising the importance of continuity, reduce the negative impact of change on the child's developmental progress.

Because there is scope for much improvement in practice it is easy to overlook the importance of the policy framework within which practitioners operate, as well as demographic changes in society over which they have no control. Increasing numbers of lone parents, dispersal of extended families, changes in income support rules, withdrawal of benefit from 16 and 17-year olds, limits on local authority spending, even apparently unrelated economic factors such as falling farm prices, all draw more children into the care system while reducing the time and resources available to serve them. The lack of coordination between government and local authority departments which creates so many problems for parents, social workers and caregivers is supposed to be tackled by the statutory requirement for authorities to produce Children's Services Plans, but those subjected to external review have often been severely criticised (Walby, 1998). It seems very difficult to divert resources from investigative and legal work into prevention and support for families which might reduce the need for crisis work in the first place (Sanders, Jackson and Thomas, 1996; Colton, Williams and Drury, 1995). Another important factor is the constant turmoil that has characterised social work and social services departments over the past few years. The introduction of unitary authorities in Scotland, Wales and parts of England – on top of the chronic tendency of social services departments to deal with problems by reorganising themselves – has created a degree of movement and change within child care social work that not only mirrors the instability experienced by looked after children but also helps to create it. Many of the causes of instability within the care system are located at policy and management levels, but we have not found any research or analysis on the impact of policy and managerial decisions on children's movement between placements.

We write at a time when there is widespread recognition of the serious weaknesses of the child welfare service, both in its failure to protect children who have been separated from their families, often as a result of abuse and neglect, from further abuse within the system (Utting, 1997; Kent, 1997), and in its continued inability to avoid drift in care, provide ongoing support for careleavers, or achieve satisfactory outcomes for children who spend any length of time away from home. However, in other ways this is a hopeful time, when there is a real impetus for change, and a willingness on the part of government both to acknowledge failures and provide resources for improvement. The 'Quality Protects' initiative announced by the Secretary of State for Health in 1998 sets targets which include a reduction in the number of placement changes for children. Although the criterion of no more than three moves in a year is not very ambitious, it does at least show some recognition of the problem of instability and its importance. We hope that this book will make a contribution towards further raising awareness of the problem and suggesting some ways in which it might be tackled.

Selection of studies and methods of research

The aim of the 'What Works?' series is to help to make research more useful to practitioners and managers by providing a focused analysis and presentation of what has been learned about effective interventions in particular areas of social welfare. The aim is linked with the ideas of evidence-based practice (Alderson et al., 1996; Oakley and Roberts, 1996); these combine the principle that one should not intervene in people's lives without having demonstrable reasons for believing that the intervention will be helpful and effective, and the belief that there is evidence from research which can provide such reasons.

There has been considerable debate about the evidence-based approach, with some arguing that it is a misguided attempt to reduce the complexities of social work intervention to simple formulae of success and failure. It may be that the reality which can be expressed in terms of evidence-based practice does not represent the whole of what is involved in social work intervention; but this is not a reason for failing to use the approach in settings where it is appropriate. 'What works?' is a deceptively simple question, and the answer will often be rather complicated. This is certainly the case with the present book. However, anyone who intervenes in people's lives, especially those who are relatively vulnerable and powerless, has a responsibility to make full use of available knowledge about the effects of alternative kinds of intervention. It is our hope that this book will make that easier for those involved in the care of looked after children.

Research studies can be classified in several different ways, and we give a brief summary below of some of the main approaches relevant to our subject. A more detailed discussion can be found in two earlier reports in this series, *What Works in Leaving Care?* (Stein, 1997) and *What Works in the Early Years?* (Macdonald and Roberts, 1995).

Advocates of the evidence-based approach tend to argue for randomised controlled trials (RCTs) as the 'gold standard' for research studies that provide a sound basis for practice. The characteristics of a randomised controlled trial are that a particular intervention is given to some individuals in a population but not to others, and that the selection of subjects for intervention is made randomly. It is the method of choice for evaluating new drugs. Unfortunately in many areas of social welfare such trials are scarce, whether because they are out of favour among researchers or funding bodies, or more often because of inherent difficulties in conducting them. Randomised controlled trials can be difficult to set up and there may be perceived ethical problems with them in some service areas. Another serious difficulty is that much social work is highly context-sensitive, and this makes it hard either to standardise interventions or to generalise the findings of research. The context is continually changing, and many aspects of intervention are not understood well enough for controlled trials to be undertaken. Janet Lewis has pointed out that there is a demand for evaluation of new and experimental methods of intervention which are not ready for randomised trials. In this case a very practical approach to evaluation may be needed to help those carrying out the intervention but it cannot be expected to produce widely generalisable results (Lewis, 1998).

Whatever the reason, the result is that RCTs are very rare in social work with children, especially in Britain, and much social welfare research tends to take other forms. The three principal forms, all of which will feature in this book, are:

- *quasi-experimental studies* in which those receiving an intervention are compared with others who do not receive it for reasons not governed by the research – for instance because they live in another geographical area or because they do not choose to take part. Some cross-matching may take place, but the reliability and validity of such studies may be seen to be less than in a randomised controlled trial – for instance the characteristics of participants may be different in important ways from those of 'refusers'.

- *general surveys* of an area of service which look for associations between variables. Many such studies have been conducted, often on a large scale. They may be prospective or retrospective, and are sometimes combined with other methods.

- *qualitative studies* which attempt to understand the process of intervention or the experiences and perceptions of those involved (client-opinion studies). Such research is often undertaken to identify new questions or hypotheses which may then be tested by other methods, or else to add richness to data gathered by survey methods; although some researchers, influenced by contemporary social theory, see 'ethnographic' research as being of primary value (Atkinson, 1990).

In child care research in general, the majority of studies tend to be surveys or qualitative studies or a combination of the two, rather than experimental or quasi-experimental. This is certainly true of most of the research which bears on the question of stability for looked after children, and this overall balance is reflected in the selection we have made here.

While we make reference to many pieces of research, we have concentrated on a smaller number of key studies which seem to offer insights of particular value to practitioners and managers. Where it is helpful we refer to the methodology and design of the research – the size and representativeness of samples, the use of matched or control groups – and also to the strength of the findings and to whether the research has been replicated or there is other work which lends support to it.

We have made use of both quantitative and qualitative research, as well as reports of the few projects which have made stability a central aim. This is a field in which there is still a good deal of uncertainty and there are considerable gaps in knowledge, and it is important to make use of the best research of any kind which sheds light on what kinds of practices may help promote and maintain stability. Inevitably in what follows there is some overlap with Clive Sellick and June Thoburn's extremely comprehensive review of the literature on *What Works in Family Placement?* (Sellick and Thoburn, 1996). Stability *within* placement is not their main focus, but much of what they say about good practice in foster care is highly relevant to our topic, and should be read alongside this report.

Outline of the book

The purpose of this book is to ask

- what is the importance of stability in caring for children and young people away from home?

- how does it relate to other aspects of quality of care for separated children?

- what is the extent of stability and instability in the care system?

- what are the effects of instability on children's well-being and development?

- what factors assist in promoting and maintaining stability?

- what can and should we do to promote stability in the future?

In Chapter 2 we attempt to put the question of stability in context, in relation to the overall aims of the care system, to changes in emphasis in provision since the Second World War, and to developments in thinking about children and childhood in recent years. In Chapter 3 we clarify our use of the concept of stability and the associated concept of continuity. We see how an understanding of the need for continuity in care can enable us to give substance to the idea of stability and make it something more than simply staying in the same placement. In Chapter 4 we review the evidence of the extent of instability and its harmful effects, and consider some of the factors which may contribute to it. In Chapter 5 we look more closely at the evidence concerning what factors work for or against stability in different types of placement setting. In Chapter 6 we consider the interaction between stability and continuity, and examine some attempts that have been made to improve things. In Chapter 7 we report on some innovative ideas in practice. Finally, in Chapter 8 we review what we have learned about promoting and maintaining stability, in terms of its implications (a) for practitioners, (b) for managers and (c) for policy makers.

CHAPTER 2 : AIMS OF THE LOOKED AFTER SYSTEM

What is it that we want for children and young people who are looked after? Since the historic Children Act of 1948, the aim of the care system has ostensibly been to make life for children and young people as *normal* as possible. That Act, as part of the post-war settlement we call the Welfare State, introduced the idea that children might be looked after not as a punitive response to their own misbehaviour or to the inadequacy of their parents, but as a service to families – normalising as much as possible the process of coming into care. It provided for children to be returned to their families on request, unless families had shown themselves to be 'unfit', and it gave to local authorities and voluntary organisations a duty to work for the restoration of children to their families unless this was against their interests.

At the same time the Children Act tried to ensure that those children who could not return to their own families would be provided with good care and as normal a life as possible when 'in care'. Wherever children were placed, agencies had a duty to enable them to make use of services provided for children in their own families – signalling an end to the deliberate stigmatisation involved in separate provision of education, clothing, religious worship and so on. Placement with a foster family was envisaged as the placement of choice for most children, and it was expected that the use of large residential institutions, in particular, would quickly diminish. The Act had of course been preceded by the death of a child in foster care, and it introduced safeguards to ensure that children were well cared for and that the standard of care was supervised and regularly inspected. For each child a suitable family was to be identified who would care for him or her as long as needed – and who would undertake to do so as if s/he were their own child.

The 1948 Act therefore marked, in common with the other planks in the raft of social reforms which were introduced in the late 1940s, an end to the principle of 'less eligibility' which underpinned the nineteenth century version of the Poor Law. This was the principle that those who found themselves dependent on the state (or, by extension, on charity) must always be worse served than those who were able to support themselves and their families. From now on children in care were to have the same standard of care, education and maintenance as ordinary children in the community; not, perhaps, those whose parents had two houses and sent them to private schools, but at least those of the 'respectable' working class whose aspirations and self-confidence in the post-war period were probably higher than they had ever been before. Maybe some ambiguity still remained about precisely what standard of comparability was being used, and this would resurface in future years when the problems of poverty and class refused to go away; but the view that children in care were only entitled to the bare minimum for survival was no longer tenable.

If the aim of the legislation was to give to children in care a good experience of normal family life, then stability, in the sense of a child remaining in the same placement, was an important indication of success. The child who was shunted about from one place to another was not receiving good enough parenting, was not receiving the consistent care that would normally be the lot of other children in the community, and was unlikely to grow up with comparable advantages or prospects (the employability of care leavers had been a concern of the care system long before it worried much about their happiness, and it would still be so). It was during this period that the theoretical work of John Bowlby, and the practical research of the Robertsons, made professionals and policy makers acutely aware of the harm that could be done to children by separation from parental figures. These ideas later developed into the more sophisticated form of 'attachment theory' which is influential in modern social work practice (see for instance Howe, 1995; Fahlberg, 1994). Such theories can have two quite different implications for the provision of care for children and young people. On the one hand they can imply that separating children from their families is to be avoided, and that if it takes place then it is important to return them as soon as possible and to maintain links in any case. On the other hand they can imply that children who are separated need the opportunity to form new and lasting attachments with substitute carers. The tension between these two versions of attachment may be felt both in discussions of policy and in decision making in individual cases, as we shall see.

Over the fifty years since the Children Act, changes both in social services and in the wider society have had an effect on the way in which the care system provides for children – on its aims and on its success in achieving them. In the rest of this introduction we review some of these changes and their implications for the concept of stability.

Permanency, planning and outcomes

In the 1960s and early 1970s the most striking feature of child care policy and practice was the development of policies for supporting families in the community and reducing the need for children to come into care. This was followed by a period in which concern was expressed for the security and stability of children in care, exemplified by Jane Rowe and Lydia Lambert's research into 'Children Who Wait' (Rowe and Lambert, 1973) and by the Children Act 1975. The Act may be seen as a high water mark for a certain kind of concern with stability. It gave both local authorities and some foster parents power to prevent the return of children to their families once they had become settled in care, and made it easier for adoption to be arranged in the face of parental objection. However, it was not fully implemented and did little to reduce movement of children within the care system. At the same time the idea of *permanency planning* was translated to Britain from the USA in a form which emphasised the urgency of establishing permanent substitute family placements for children who could not be quickly returned home; and many agencies adopted policies which included cut-off dates for restoration work. The tension between this 'either/or' approach to planning for children, and the desire of many social workers to give parents as much chance as possible to look after their own children, was never really resolved (a problem noted by several commentators at the time; see Jackson, 1976). In the later 1980s, moreover, it was overtaken by a much more specific focus on the process of making and reviewing plans for children, following research which drew attention to the absence of clear planning, the lack of partnership between agencies and families, and 'drift' in the care system (Department of Health and Social Security, 1985a).

The Children Act 1989, followed by the Children (Scotland) Act 1995 and the Children (Northern Ireland) Order 1995, came during a period in which there was a growing preoccupation with assessment and planning in social services, and a general concern with participation and accountability in all public services. This is reflected in the emphasis which the Act has placed on formal procedures for planning and reviewing, with clear specification of what is to be considered and who is to be involved, including of course children and their parents. At the same time there has also been a growing unease about *outcomes* for children and young people who are looked after. Research which shows poor educational achievement and often poor health, combined with evidence of the poverty and distress often suffered by young people who have left the care system, has led to a coordinated attempt to develop ways to measure and improve every aspect of the *parenting* provided for separated children (Jackson, 1987, 1989, Parker et al., 1991; Ward, 1995, Jackson and Kilroe, 1996). Related to the concern for outcomes is the explosion of concern with child abuse, both as a reason for a child coming into care or accommodation and as a danger once he or she is in care. Finally, the same period has seen a steady move away from residential to foster care and toward the semi-professionalisation of foster care, with implications which we discuss in a later chapter.

The question of how *stability* is provided for children and young people by the care system has to be seen in the context of these other concerns with planning and with outcomes. Stability is not necessarily to be identified with 'permanence'; for many of the children looked after by local authorities and voluntary organisations permanence will not be an issue, but stability will. It continues to be a measure of how well the planning process is working, and of how successfully the system is producing desired outcomes for children. As well as being an important element in individual planning for children, stability can therefore be a performance indicator for the system in its managerial aspect – for example by the Department of Health in its 'Quality Protects' initiative as we mentioned earlier.

An important development in the 1990s has been an increased interest in the management of the child care system and also in its cost effectiveness. One can draw a distinction between an individualised approach to caring for separated children, which focuses on each child's needs for health, development and autonomy, and a managerial approach which highlights the system's demands for efficiency and cost effectiveness. Drawing the distinction poses the question to what extent these approaches work in the same direction, and what happens if they are in contradiction. Does managerialism threaten children's stability – for instance by closing 'uneconomic' establishments, or by insisting on foster carers sticking to the tasks for which they are approved – while an individualised approach protects it; or, on the other hand, is a managerial systems approach the only way to ensure that planning in individual cases is delivering the goods for children? In their different ways the 'Looking After Children' project and the Dartington Social Research Unit's exercise in 'Matching Needs and Services' (DSRU,undated) represent attempts to bring the two together.

Thinking about children

It is also important to take account of recent changes in the theoretical context of work with children and young people. Research continues into the effects of childhood trauma and disruption, and there is a growing interest in and investigation of 'resilience' (Haggerty et al. 1996, Fraser 1997, Rutter 1997). Gradually we are learning more about the precise effects on children of adverse life events including abuse – now the most common reason for children to come into care for extended periods – as well as separation and loss. We are also learning more about children's ability to overcome adversity and do well in later life, and the importance of stable relationships in achieving this (Jackson and Martin, 1998).

Both in sociology and in psychology there is more understanding of and interest in children as *social actors*, as subjects rather than objects both of social activity and of social research. Children are increasingly seen as active participants in their own upbringing rather than as the passive objects of 'socialisation' or development. These theoretical developments are linked with political developments in the shape of a much greater awareness of children's rights. The adoption of the United Nations Convention on the Rights of the Child in 1989 was a key moment in this respect, but not the only one. Several countries have legislated for children to have the right not to be hit, for example, or the right to have their views considered by parents and others before decisions are made which affect their lives. Several countries have introduced children's commissioners or Ombudsmen, and there are demands for a similar office in the UK.

Taken together, these developments represent a change in how children are perceived and thus have consequences for how we plan, provide and evaluate child care services and for what criteria of success we use. The implications of the 'Gillick' judgement which recognised that children have some autonomy in the face of parental control, and of the limited but significant rights of participation given to children in the Children Act 1989, the Children (Northern Ireland) Order 1995 and the Children (Scotland) Act 1995, are still being worked out in policy and practice. However, there is clearly no going back to a time when decisions about the future of children in care were routinely made without reference to their own wishes and feelings.

The importance of stability

What is the place of stability in the midst of all these other concerns, and what effect have these changes had on the stability of care and placement for looked after children? At times it has seemed as if the issue of stability in care has been overshadowed by a preoccupation with systems for planning, with the specification of needs and professionalisation of services, with 'partnership' or latterly with the child's voice. However, the question of stability has refused to go away, and some of the developments in services and in thinking in the last twenty years have perhaps enabled us to understand the question better and put it into a clearer perspective.

Key points from Chapter 2

- Since 1948 the purpose of the care system has been to give children as normal a life as possible, and to aim for 'good parenting'.

- During the post-war years the focus of concern in child care policy has shifted several times, from the aim of preventing reception into care, to a preoccupation with providing secure long-term placements, to a concentration on dealing with abuse.

- In recent years the focus on the process of planning and on partnership with families has tended to eclipse the issue of stability, although now the development of outcome measures is beginning to reinstate stability as an important objective of care.

- There is a tension between managerial and systems approaches to child care services and an individualised or case-based approach. Both approaches can work for and against stability.

- We are learning more about the resilience of children and the factors which enable them to overcome adversity.

- There is increasing awareness of children's need and right to participate in decisions about their own lives.

CHAPTER 3 : STABILITY, CONTINUITY AND CHILDREN'S NEEDS

Aspects of stability

This chapter asks what we mean by 'stability' and why it is important. We make three important qualifications to the use of the concept of stability in discussing what works in child care. These are to do with continuity, with children's needs generally, and with the question of long- and short-term objectives.

At the simplest level, stability can be defined as merely remaining in the same place or with the same people. In itself this may often be of considerable importance to a child's well-being; for a homeless or refugee child, or one whose experience is of being 'shunted around' from one carer to another, to settle down in one place must be a major step forward.

However, this hardly represents the summit of our aspirations for children who are looked after. A child may be in a stable situation but have substantial unmet needs; and there may be instances when the 'stability' in itself is in conflict with other aims or values. There is little benefit to a child in remaining in the same placement if s/he is unhappy there or if her/his other basic needs are not being met. It is arguable that situations such as those which Jane Rowe and Lydia Lambert discovered years ago, of children who remain in foster or residential homes when they should be moving either back home or on to more permanent placements, could count as situations of stability – but they are clearly not in children's interests. Likewise a child who remains for years in an unsuitable residential establishment because of a failure to secure parental agreement for a move to foster care may be getting 'stability' at the expense of being deprived of the kind of care that would really meet his or her needs. Another child may be allowed to remain in an inappropriate foster home without developing real attachments, when his or her interests would perhaps be better served by confronting the fact that another placement could offer more.

All this is a way of saying that successful outcomes for looked after children are not one-dimensional, and while stability of placement is an important factor it is not the only one. Furthermore, stability itself may be multi-dimensional. A child may remain in the same placement but experience breakdowns in relationships, loss of contact with friends, or repeated changes of social worker – all of these are instances of instability. A child whose schooling is interrupted by periods of exclusion or unnecessary changes of school, or whose health care is disrupted by failure to ensure continuity of oversight, is suffering from instability in key areas of life. A child whose sense of identity is threatened or undermined, perhaps by a lack of contact with their own culture or history, can also be seen as affected by instability.

We could therefore decide to use a concept of stability that reflects this multi-dimensional character and encompasses different elements of a child's situation. We might separate out the idea of stability into the following separate aspects:

Stability of placement would mean not only that the child remains in the same placement, but also that the placement continues to offer reliable care and support from trusted people in a predictable way, and that it is seen by those involved as a stable setting in which the child can grow up or remain as long as needed.

Stability of relationships would mean the child being part of a network of family and social relationships, both in the place where s/he lives and outside, which remain stable and continuous over time. This includes not just the child's relationships with their household and kinship group, which for most of us tend to be extremely stable, but also relationships with friends which may be more fluid or subject to change. 'Stability' would imply that such change should follow the child's inclinations and not be forced by other circumstances.

Stability of education implies a continuity in the provision of opportunities for learning that are geared to the child's interests and aptitudes, in a context in which regular plans and assessments are employed in order to ensure that what is provided will maximise the child's opportunities to learn and develop and contribute to educational success in the future.

Stability of health care would mean that the child receives services which are based on a knowledge and regard for the child as an individual and any particular needs s/he has, and which incorporate regular and appropriate surveillance to ensure that this continues to be the case.

Stability of community implies that the child remains part of a living community or neighbourhood, and that there is continuity in the child's membership of a cultural reference group which is recognisably theirs.

Stability of personal identity would refer to the need of each of us for an abiding sense of who we are, what we are like, what we are called, where we belong and what are our goals and values.

Stability and continuity

Clearly there are links and overlaps between all these aspects of stability – and in particular the last, 'stability of personal identity', is in some measure dependent on all the others. However, the above distinctions seem to be important and worth making. We would argue that a multi-dimensional conception of stability such as this could be a useful tool in guiding child care research and in evaluating practice, and we did seriously consider using such a model in this book.

On reflection we decided that for our present purposes it is worth more clearly delineating stability of placement from the other aspects identified here. Many of the questions we will be asking, and much of the research we will be considering, relate specifically to discovering which factors tend to promote stability in this more narrow sense, and it will be important to have a working concept which enables us to focus on this. On the other hand the other important aspects of stability which we identified above must not be forgotten. We have therefore chosen to distinguish between stability and continuity, using *stability* to refer to a child's remaining in the same placement and *continuity* to mean all the other things that we have identified as important in terms of relationships, identity and care. This is the conceptual framework that we will use in this book. *Stability* will therefore be used to mean a child staying in the same place or with the same people, while *continuity* will be applied to the child's networks of relationships, their personal and cultural identity, and their education and health care.

Clearly one should not overstate the contradictions between these aspects of stability and continuity, because in many cases they will go together. The child who remains in the same place with the same people is in general more likely to enjoy continuity of relationships, community and identity, and of education and health care, than a child who experiences a series of moves. However, the connection is not a necessary one, and drawing the distinction may help us to be observant of the situations when stability and continuity do not go together and may even be at odds with each other. We cannot take it for granted that in providing a child with basic stability we are thereby meeting all of her or his needs for continuity, while on the other hand it is possible to preserve continuity in at least some aspects of a child's life even when a change of placement is unavoidable.

Stability and children's needs

A further complication, when we come to look at measures of success and failure in child placement, is that neither 'stability' nor 'continuity' covers everything that we might be aiming for. As we suggested at the beginning of this chapter, a child may remain in a 'stable' placement that is far from meeting his or her needs, or that is actually counter-productive in some if not all respects. Not all placements deserve to be maintained, and sometimes a placement may need to be brought to an end in order to ensure that children get the quality of care to which they are entitled.

In assessing the success of services and systems for looking after children, it is important to attend to processes and to outcomes as fully as possible, bearing in mind the range of children's needs. Children do not come into the care system simply because they need accommodation. They may have needs for particular kinds of care, for educational or therapeutic input, as a result of the circumstances which led to their needing to be looked after. They will also have continuing needs unrelated to those circumstances, because they are who they are or simply because they are children – needs for friendship, for social development, for cultural or sporting activities, for religious expression. They will have their own views about what they want and need, which may or may not coincide with the views of parents or professionals – and they are entitled to express those views and have them heard. These needs cannot all be subsumed under the heading of 'stability'.

What we would argue is that stability is an important indicator of success in meeting children's needs, indeed one of the most important; but that it must be used in association with other indicators. The kinds of measures that have been developed in the 'Looking After Children' package, in relation to the several dimensions of health, education, emotional development, social presentation and so on, enable a broader view to be taken of the care which children are given and the outcomes which might be desired (Ward, 1995, Jackson and Kilroe, 1996). It would be easy to focus on placement stability to the exclusion of these other factors, in part because it is relatively easy to measure. However, it would be regrettable if this resulted in placement moves being resisted on the occasions when they are actually in children's best interests.

In the following chapters we will refer from time to time to these other indicators; even when we do not, all that we say about the factors that appear to promote stability must be read in the light of this qualification; that stability on its own is not the end of the story, but at best the beginning.

Stability in the long term and in the short term

The third qualification we want to make at the outset has to do with questions of timescale. In focusing on 'stability' we have found that it is deceptively easy to concentrate on issues to do with permanence, with long-term substitute families, or with eventual return home. These questions are important and often intriguing, and will rightly occupy much of our attention in this book. However, they ought not to be pursued without also considering the thousands of children who pass through the care system more briefly. Stability and continuity are also important issues, we contend, for these children. For a child who is in the care system for only six months, it may make a huge difference whether that six months is spent in one family or in a series of different settings. It may also make a difference whether they are able to continue at the same school, see the same doctor, spend time with the same group of friends, or attend the same clubs.

In thinking about what works in promoting and maintaining stability for looked after children we will therefore consider evidence that relates to patterns in short-term care as well as long-term outcomes. In the long run, as Keynes memorably said, we are all dead; what happens from day to day, especially in childhood, is very often the most pressing reality of life. As we shall see, there is some evidence of things that can be done to help ensure that those children who have brief experiences of the care system also benefit from stability.

What counts as stability?

In this book we will therefore be looking at stability as far as we can in this multi-dimensional way. At times we will be attending to relatively simple indicators such as the number of moves a child experiences, or the length of time s/he remains in the same place. We will consider the causes and effects of longer or shorter stays, of more or fewer moves, during children's time in the care system. We will also look at the extent to which children find placements which are genuinely permanent, either with their original families or with new ones. At other times, however, we will try to relate this information to what is known about other kinds of stability and continuity, and to the success of agencies and placement services in meeting children's many other needs.

Continuity and outcomes

Nearly all the empirical research on children in care carried out in the 1980s was concerned with continuation or premature ending of placements, with decision-making about placement, or the relative merits of different kinds of placement. There was almost none concerned with other kinds of outcomes, and a curious unwillingness to confront the evidence that children in care appeared to lag behind others in their development and usually had a poor quality of life in adulthood.

The Department of Health Working Party which initiated the development of the Looking After Children project, identified lack of continuity as a major factor in the poor outcomes for children who spent any length of time in care (Parker et al, 1991). There were several different kinds of discontinuity. First there was the lack of continuity of *information*. Local authorities used dozens of different forms to record facts about children received into care, kept in different places and rarely accessible at short notice. Case-recording was erratic and important information about a child changing placement was often not conveyed to the new carer. Information not recorded at the time of the first placement might often be lost forever. Secondly there was discontinuity of care in the sense that no one person had an overview of the child and his or her needs over time. And thirdly there was discontinuity of the child's experience, being cut off from family, friends, their past, their school.

The Looking After Children system, now implemented in almost all UK local authorities, addresses continuity at two levels. The administrative forms record essential information about the child and his/her history, family, previous placements and care plan. The age-related Assessment and Action Records specify desirable outcomes for the child on key dimensions of development and ask questions to find out if the necessary 'parental' actions are being taken to achieve them. The dimensions were chosen to cover those aspects of children's lives which parents consider most important, and also those which research has shown to be particularly problematic for looked after children, namely Health, Education, Family and Social Relationships, Identity, Behavioural and Emotional Development, Social Presentation and Self-Care Skills (see Jackson, 1998, for a more detailed account).

Research undertaken in the course of developing the LAC materials showed that placement changes without close attention to continuity led to many deficits in the care of looked after children, for example poor health care, even at the most basic level of ensuring immunisations were carried out, chronic health problems not treated and dental appointments not made or kept (Ward, 1995). A move could have a disastrous effect on the child's education at all ages, resulting in long periods out of school, a plunge in attainment, disruption of examination courses. Repeated moves made a good school adjustment almost impossible, which in turn increased the instability of the placement. All children, not only those from minority ethnic groups, might have their sense of identity threatened by lack of knowledge about their background and history. Contact with relatives, previous carers and friends was often lost. Children were bewildered by different rules and expectations in different placements. In the absence of consistent care they did not have the opportunity to learn gradually how to look after themselves and their environment as children in their own homes do.

The Looking After Children materials are not of course a panacea but they do make a practical attempt to create greater continuity in children's everyday lives, and to identify what needs to be done to promote their satisfactory development, which may in turn contribute to stability of placement.

Key points from Chapter 3

● Stability is not the only important factor in the lives of children who are looked after. It is not in a child's interest to remain in a placement that is not meeting his or her needs, simply for the sake of stability.

● Stability can be seen as a multi-dimensional concept, encompassing not only placement but other important aspects of a child's life.

- In this book we distinguish between *stability* and *continuity:*

  - 'stability' means a child staying in the same place or with the same people;

  - 'continuity' applies to the child's education and health care, networks of relationships, and their personal and cultural identity

- In assessing the extent to which services are meeting children's needs, it is important to use stability alongside a range of other indicators.

- Stability is not just a long-term issue – children who remain in the care system for short periods also deserve a stable experience while they are accommodated.

- Continuity must be addressed as an issue in itself. The Looking After Children materials are an essential tool for recording information and ensuring that all important dimensions of a child's life receive due attention.

CHAPTER 4 : EFFECTS AND CAUSES OF INSTABILITY

Moving house is well known to be one of life's most stressful experiences, following closely behind bereavement and divorce. In fact one of the women interviewed by Audrey McCollum for her book *The Trauma of Moving* (McCollum, 1990) said 'Moving is like dying. It's a kind of death. It's coming to an end' (p.85), and it was a parallel drawn by many of her other subjects. If even one move is felt so intensely, what must it be like to suffer this experience over and over again, like so many looked after children?

The literature on moving house, because it is usually based on research with adults who have more words to express their feelings and griefs than children do, can provide many insights into what can make the losses easier to bear. One finding with important implications for child care practice is that those who feel the move was their own choice find it less distressing than if the move was imposed on them.

> If there is a single characteristic that distinguishes those who benefit from mobility from those who lose from it, it is the degree of choice they have. People who benefit are those who, because of their resources and knowledge, can choose whether to move or not, and where to move.
>
> (Fischer and Stueve, 1977, p.182)

It is hardly necessary to point out that looked after children seldom have any real choice about when or where to move, even if they are consulted. Nigel Thomas and Claire O'Kane (1998) in their research on children's involvement in decision-making found that, although children were more likely to be included in reviews than in the past, they often had little say in decisions about placement. Research on the impact of moving on individual well-being has identified whether the move is voluntary or involuntary as the most important variable: 'for those whose forced moves involve more radical environmental changes...the relocation may literally be lethal' (Bourestom 1984, p.67). This is well recognized in the case of older people moved from home to residential care, but less so in the case of children, whose wounds may be internal.

When adults or children living in their own family move from one house or community to another they normally do so in the company of familiar people and take with them at least some of their furniture and possessions, so that they can begin at once to create a feeling of home in their new setting. Even so, quite severe physical and psychological reactions are often reported: grief, depression, anxiety, isolation, loss of identity, low self-esteem, distortions of mood, chronic illness, marital breakdown. Children who move to a new foster or residential home not only have to adjust to an unfamiliar place, they may at the same time lose everything that gives them a sense of security and rootedness in their everyday lives. They lose their daily contact with significant adults with whom they may have formed a close relationship, their friends, their school, leisure activities, and sometimes treasured possessions which connect them with their past. Some of these losses can be avoided or mitigated, as we suggest in Chapter 6, by awareness of the vital importance of continuity, but others cannot, and for some children moving will always be traumatic and carry a high risk of psychological damage.

Attachment and loss

Attachment theory would predict that a child who has experienced even one extended separation from a primary caregiver is at risk of psychological ill-effects. When this experience is repeated many times the child is placed in a state of chronic insecurity and learns not to form attachments or relationships in order to avoid the pain of losing them. New carers then see the child as cold and unresponsive. John Bowlby, in his last published work (Bowlby, 1991) pointed to the significance of empirical findings on the different patterns of communication between infants and their mothers, depending on whether the infants were classified as 'secure' or 'insecure-avoidant', when they were frustrated, frightened or distressed. In contrast to the secure infants, the more distressed the insecurely attached children became, the less they communicated. When the same children were interviewed at the age of ten, these differences persisted. The secure children said they would turn to a parent if they were sad, afraid or angry, the insecure-avoidant children were more likely to keep their feelings to themselves. Bowlby suggests that in adulthood the ability or inability to express thoughts and feelings to others and to seek their comfort and help is a crucial variable distinguishing those who can continue to function in adversity and those who succumb to mental illness. The violent and aggressive behaviour displayed by some children in care placements can readily be understood as a distorted attempt to communicate, though this does not necessarily help their carers to cope with it (Cairns, 1999). These children are at high risk of ending up in secure accommodation, where the majority of residents have been through a large number of different placements and have suffered from discontinuity of care resulting in a wide range of educational and health problems (Social Work Services Inspectorate for Scotland, 1996).

We do not know how many children who remain in long-term care are likely to have experienced secure attachment in infancy, but it is almost certainly a minority. This makes it more difficult for them to become attached to substitute carers, or even to form close relationships with them, but paradoxically it also reduces their capacity to deal with loss and separation. Rosalind Folman points out that the majority of children entering care do so with a model of adults as uncaring and not trustworthy, and therefore it is much more difficult for them to use foster parents as sources of comfort than for children who have had secure attachments in early childhood. She suggests that previous research has neglected a crucial element in placement outcome, that is how the children themselves understand and cope with their situation (Folman, 1998). It is remarkable that so many children do, nevertheless, form warm, loving relationships with new carers. The extraordinary resilience displayed by children adopted from the appalling conditions of Romanian 'orphanages', which is discussed in Chapter 6, is a reminder that we should never give up hope (Rutter et al., 1998).

Movement within the care system

It is difficult to know if instability within care has increased, because there is so little firm information on the subject; however, almost all studies show a high rate of placement turnover, not confined to children with 'special needs' (which often means no more than particularly difficult behaviour). Placement instability is not a uniquely British problem. The few American studies which have addressed the phenomenon of placement change also report a great deal of movement within care (Fein, Maluccio and Kluger, 1990, Staff and Fein, 1995), though not as much as in this country.

Jane Rowe and colleagues' massive survey of admissions to care, discharges and moves in six local authorities (Rowe, Hundleby and Garnett, 1989) was carried out in the mid–1980s, before the Children Act 1989, and only measured moves over a 12–23 month period. Over half (57%) of the cohort of 2010 children with at least one admission in the first year of the study had no moves, 26 per cent had one, 9 per cent had two and 8 per cent three or more. But 2 per cent (38 children) had five or more moves over this short time, including six pre-schoolers. There were some differences between authorities, with the lowest having 6 per cent of children with three or more moves, and the highest 11 per cent. The age group 5–10 was the most stable, three quarters having one or two placements, whereas over half the adolescents who came into care as offenders had at least three placements, except for 16-year olds in penal establishments, who tended to stay there.

This was an entirely statistical study based on questionnaires completed by social workers, but the authors point out how misleading a straight counting of moves may be. For example 'how can one compare the move to a foster family for a child who has spent three nights in a children's home after being admitted in an emergency with a move into a residential establishment after a long-term foster home breakdown?' (Rowe et al, 1989, p.48). The impact of a single move on a child's sense of security may be far greater than two or three changes of placement that are clearly intended to be transitional. Nevertheless the extent of movement reported in this large-scale study compares favourably with more recent research and even with other studies carried out at about the same time.

Other information on stability comes from selected care populations, in particular young people participating in leaving care schemes. One would expect them to have had a less stable care experience than other careleavers, because if they were able to return home or had had successful long term foster placements they would be less likely to need support from a special scheme. Biehal, Clayden, Stein and Wade (1995) studied 74 young people in leaving care schemes in three contrasting areas. Just over half had entered care as teenagers, and the remainder at all ages from infancy upwards. Only one in ten had remained in the same placement throughout their care career and the same percentage moved more than ten times. 52% had between one and three moves, and nearly a third had moved four or more times. This pattern of movement and disruption was similar to the findings of Millham, Bullock and Hosie (1986) and Berridge and Cleaver (1987) with more representative care populations. The Dartington Social Research Unit's study of children returning home from care found that of those who stayed away for two years or more 84 per cent moved placement at least once and 56 per cent moved two or more times (Bullock et al, 1993). The young people who had many moves, categorised by Biehal et al as 'unsettled', tended to continue the pattern of instability and frequent movement after care, which boded ill for their quality of life in adulthood.

David Berridge and Isabelle Brodie (1998) attempted to compare the situation of 70 young people living in children's homes with the similar population in Berridge's 1985 study. They found that children were much less likely to stay long in public care, almost half having been away from home for under a year. In adolescent homes three-fifths of the residents had been present less than three months. The proportion of fostering breakdowns and moves within care was less than in the earlier study, but the average number of placements for adolescents, despite the short time they had been looked after, was 3.3, and a third had already lived in five or more different settings. Because of the difference in length of time in care the figures are not directly comparable. However, it does seem that children who are not already in a well-functioning long-term foster home when they enter adolescence are especially vulnerable to serial placement breakdown (Sinclair, Garnett, and Berridge, 1995; Triseliotis, Borland, Hill and Lambert, 1995), or what John Brown, in a report on adolescent and family support services discussed later, has memorably called 'accommodation pinball'.

Although the risk of extreme instability is greatest for adolescents, children who enter care at an earlier age cannot rely on a stable care experience either. Distressing examples abound; for instance a survey among Barnardo's establishments in Scotland found that 21 per cent of the children had experienced six or more moves before coming to their current placement – including one child of primary school age who had moved 40 times (Hughes, 1996) – and in another unit there was a boy aged 13 who was found to have had 52 changes of placement. The Looking After Children team, comparing 204 children in care placements with 379 children living in the community, commented on the fact that the looked after group had experienced on average at least three moves since admission, whereas nearly all the home-based children had lived with at least one parent all their lives and 37 per cent had always lived at the same address (Ward, 1995).

Nor do young people who are relatively unproblematic and have done well despite spending several years in care seem much more likely to have a stable care career. In Sonia Jackson's study of 'high achievers' – careleavers who had gone on to further or higher education – the average number of placement moves for boys was 3 and for girls 5.5 (Jackson and Martin, 1998). Among the comparison group of careleavers who had not been educationally successful, the boys had had 5.7 moves on average and the girls 4.4. In both groups there were several individuals who had experienced more than 20 moves, and the most extreme case was a woman who, on obtaining access to her case file, discovered that she had been moved 36 times during her life in care.

Another recent indication of the degree of movement comes from a questionnaire survey of over 2000 looked after children carried out by the Who Cares? Trust. The study found that for those in care for five years or more, only one in ten had remained in one placement and nearly a quarter had been in 11 or more different placements. Age made little difference: 9 per cent of the eleven and under age group had moved more than 10 times, almost half of the whole group had had between 2 and 5 placements and 17 per cent between 6 and 10. As in other studies, those in more restrictive placements had the most disrupted care histories: young people in secure units were less likely than other respondents to have spent over five years in care, but more likely to have had many changes and moves concentrated into a shorter period before they eventually reached secure accommodation (Shaw, 1998). Despite the difficulty in comparing disparate samples, it seems probable that these figures represent a real increase in the instability of care since Jane Rowe's survey (Rowe et al, 1989). Earlier researchers would presumably have drawn attention to individuals having experienced the shockingly large number of moves recorded above had they come across them.

This is borne out by the most recent statistics from the Department of Health, which record that 20% of children looked after by local authorities in England on 31 March 1997 – 10,300 children in all – had experienced three or more placements *in the course of the previous year*. It is estimated that about 2,000 of them had six or more placements in this period (Department of Health, 1998c). As the government White Paper comments in reporting these figures, 'a settled life for a child in such circumstances is impossible' (Secretary of State for Health, 1998).

Rather more encouraging is a report by Nigel Thomas and Celia Beckett (1994) on a study of children awaiting permanent placement in one local authority, which was originally carried out in 1989 and repeated in 1992. On each occasion the authors looked at all children aged between 4 and 12 who were identified as needing permanent placement – 36 on the first occasion, 31 on the second. In contrast to the evidence quoted in Chapter 3 this research showed a marked improvement in the situations of the children on the second occasion in terms of stability:

- In 1989 the children had spent on average 2½ years in care without a settled placement; in 1992 they had been waiting on average 12 months since first coming into care or accommodation, and 6 months since the need for a permanent placement had been identified.

- In 1989 three of the children had experienced a long-term breakdown; in 1992 only one child had been in a long-term placement which had broken down.

- In 1989 sibling groups had regularly been separated in care; in 1992 only one pair of siblings had been separated, and strenuous efforts were still being made to place them together.

- In 1989 two thirds of the children had experienced changes of short-term placement, and two had moved 6 times; in 1992 two thirds had remained in the same short-term placement, and none had moved more than twice.

In looking at changes in local authority practice that might have produced such different patterns of care experience, the authors noticed that shortly after the 1989 research the local authority had embarked on a development strategy for foster care (funded by a shift in resources from residential care). Specialist family placement teams were established in each geographical division, a major recruitment campaign was undertaken, and allowances to foster carers were increased to a level significantly above NFCA recommended minimum rates. Following the introduction of the 1988 foster care regulations all foster carers' approval was reviewed and a significant number ceased to foster as a result. There were indications that a more focused and better resourced service was producing improvements both in placement choice and in support to foster carers. At the same time more emphasis was placed on assessment and planning for children in anticipation of Children Act implementation, with a training programme commissioned from Margaret Bryer based on her work on planning in child care (Bryer, 1988). It seemed likely that a combination of these developments had contributed to the improvements which the researchers noted in short-term stability for looked-after children (Thomas and Beckett, 1994).

An overview of factors associated with instability

A number of factors have been found by researchers to be associated with placement stability and instability, especially in foster care.

- Age has been identified repeatedly as an important factor (Trasler, 1960; Parker, 1966; George, 1970; Rowe et al., 1984;Thoburn et al., 1986; Berridge and Cleaver, 1987; Borland, 1991; Fratter et al., 1991). The most frequent finding is that the older the child, or the older at placement, the more likely the placement is to end prematurely. However, the findings are quite inconsistent on this point, with several studies finding middle childhood the most vulnerable stage. Berridge and Cleaver found ages six to eleven to be the period of highest risk, while for Borland it was eleven to twelve and in June Thoburn's study it was twelve to fourteen.

- Relatively recent placements are especially vulnerable, in that more break down in the first year than at any time subsequently (George, 1970; Berridge and Cleaver, 1987; Fratter et al., 1991).

- Placements where the carers have children of their own, especially if they are close in age to the child placed, are more likely to fail (Trasler, 1960; Parker, 1966; George, 1970; Berridge and Cleaver, 1987). This is a consistent finding, with the exception of Cairns and Cairns (1989) in the rather special circumstances of the Children's Family Trust (see Chapter 7).

- Children separated from their own siblings are more likely to experience breakdown (Berridge and Cleaver, 1987) This was not supported by Rowe et al. (1989), but several other studies have suggested that placing children either with their siblings, or in households where there are other foster children, may enhance stability (Parker, 1966; Berridge and Cleaver, 1987; Fratter et al., 1991).

- The child's behaviour has been regularly identified as a key factor (for example Parker, 1966, Aldgate and Hawley, 1986, and recently Palmer, 1996) However, classifications of behaviour can be extremely subjective and situation-specific, reflecting the perceptions of social workers and carers, and in the case of social workers may be second-hand. Fratter's criterion, therefore, is that the child is *described* as having behavioural difficulties or emotional problems (Fratter et al., 1991). Fratter and her colleagues also found that having a history of deprivation or abuse, or being *described* as institutionalised, appeared to be risk factors.

- Legal status: Berridge and Cleaver (1987) found that children on care orders were more likely to experience breakdown, but this was not supported by Jane Rowe's study.

- Exclusion of natural parents from placements (Berridge and Cleaver, 1987). A recent study in Hong Kong of over 800 placements found that successful reunification was also more likely if parents were involved not only in contact but in the child's daily life and routine (Tam and Ho, 1996). On the broader question of contact with birth families the evidence is less clear, and David Quinton and his colleagues have recently sounded a cautionary note (Quinton et al., 1998).

- Poor coordination of services, resource difficulties, and in particular, very hurried placements are, not surprisingly, associated with instability.

- Several studies have found that transracial placements, especially placements of mixed-parentage children with white families, appear more likely to fail – although the relationship is not a strong one (Berridge and Cleaver, 1987; Charles, Rashid and Thoburn, 1992). There is no evidence that this is true of adoptive placements.

Factors contributing to stability

When Triseliotis, Sellick, and Short (1995) reviewed the evidence relating to successful outcomes in foster care, they found that placement stability was the main indicator used. The authors distinguish between 'child factor', 'foster home factors', 'social worker factors' and 'parent factors'. A number of studies have suggested that factors in social work and agency practice can contribute towards stability of placement. Berridge and Cleaver (1987) found that a short period in residential care before a foster placement could enhance long-term stability, although a long period of residential care had the opposite effect (see also Parker 1966). It is difficult to know how to interpret these findings without detailed information on the individual circumstances, but possibly an interval of relative calm after the turmoil of admission to accommodation may help the child to recover emotional equilibrium and reduce the stress on the future foster carers. Another finding relevant to practice was that previous acquaintance between the child and the carers tended to produce more stable placements.

Aldgate and Hawley, 1986 also suggest that preparation before a foster placement is important. Of course this has long been accepted as good practice but can be difficult to achieve when so many placements are made in a situation of urgency. Berridge and Cleaver (1987) found that negotiation before breakdown and timely inputs from social workers helped to prevent problems from developing into crises. Palmer (1996) found that parental involvement in preparation for a placement promoted success.

Age and experience of carers have been frequently associated with greater stability by a number of researchers (Trasler, 1960; George, 1970; Berridge and Cleaver, 1987; Rowe et al., 1989).

In the remainder of this chapter we look more closely at some of the most important studies of stability and at their key findings, and at one very recent study. Finally we consider what we call 'institutional instability'.

Early studies of instability

Most research into placement stability and instability has been undertaken in foster care, and three pioneering studies from the 1960s are still worth noting.

Gordon Trasler (1960) traced the experiences of 138 foster children in one Children's Department: 57 whose placements had 'broken down' over a 3-year survey period and a control group of 81 children deemed to be satisfactorily placed. He discovered that placements tended to end early on; three-quarters of all breakdowns took place within the first two years. Four key variables were significantly related to outcome: (1) placement failure was more likely for children who had been separated from their parents during infancy and lived in a residential setting; (2) placements involving older children were more likely to end prematurely; (3) foster mothers aged in their early forties were more likely to make successful placements; (4) failure rates were noticeably higher when foster parents had a child of their own of the same sex and close in age to the foster child (although when another foster child was in the household the placement was more likely to continue).

Roy Parker (1966) looked back on the experiences of 209 children in planned long-stay foster placements over a five-year period, in a single Children's Department. He found that 52 per cent of placements survived for five years, and that six factors were strongly associated with outcome: (1) age at separation from mother (later separation was associated with breakdown); (2) previous care history (a previous family placement, especially if positive, or a brief spell in residential care was associated with stability, while a longer residential stay predicted instability); (3) death of mother prior to fostering (closely linked to breakdown); (4) age at placement (directly linked with breakdown); (5) behaviour problems (linked with breakdown); (6) foster parents who had children of their own (linked with breakdown, particularly if they were younger than five or close in age to the foster child).

Victor George (1970) studied foster placements in three local authorities, collecting data on 128 children from questionnaires and case records. He found that only 40% of placements lasted five years, and that they were particularly vulnerable in the first year. The children most likely to experience breakdown were: (1) children from families with a history of intervention from welfare agencies; (2) children who were older when separated from their mothers; (3) children who were older at the time of placement; (4) children with younger foster mothers; (5) children placed with foster parents who had their own children (regardless of age); (6) oddly, children whose religious faith was similar to that of their foster parents.

Foster home breakdown

David Berridge and Hedy Cleaver (1987) made an extensive study of foster placements in three local authorities. In relation to long term placement they found an incidence of 'breakdown' similar to that found in the earlier studies by Trasler, Parker and George. However, the rate of breakdown varied between agencies, mainly because of variation in the use of placement with relatives, where the breakdown rate was very low – 2 of 25 placements in the first year, none in succeeding years. There was a pattern of early placement breakdown: 'Of all planned long-term placements that eventually broke down, 40 per cent were terminated during the first year; half of these occurring within the first three months' (p.59); suggesting that intensive social work support at the early stage of placement is important. Fostering breakdowns did not normally lead to the reuniting of families: 'if anything, children were further distanced from their families... by the process of breakdown of a long-term foster placement' (p.60). The majority of placements that broke down were perceived by social workers as generally satisfactory (36%) or partly satisfactory (42%), although in a third of cases breakdown was predicted. The reasons for breakdown were 'placement-focused' in 30% of cases, 'child and placement' in 37%, 'child' alone in only 20%. This contrasts with some other studies which appear to emphasise child-focused reasons. Sex and ethnicity were not significant factors in breakdown rates, 'although there was some tendency for mixed race children placed with white, long-term foster parents to experience more breakdowns than one might expect by chance' (p.67). Age was a factor, but not as marked as in some studies; the highest rate of breakdown was in the 6–11 group. Legal status was 'one of the strongest indicators of outcome that we were able to discover' with 21% breakdown in voluntary care and 44% on care orders. According to the authors 'these findings suggest that placements that are brought about by involving natural parents in care plans have a better prognosis' (p.70), though it could also be that children on care orders tend to be more disturbed and difficult to look after. This research did not support Trasler and Parker's findings that early rearing history is a factor in subsequent stability. Longer periods in care were associated with higher likelihood of breakdown. Placements preceded by residential care did better (34%) than those from home or from fostering (51%); a period of less than a year seemed most favourable. The authors can only speculate as to the reasons behind this finding.

Berridge and Cleaver emphasise the importance of preparation for long-term placement; previous acquaintance between child and carer was associated with stability and very hurried placements with instability. Social networks also seemed important: contact with families, continuity of school, and supportive relationships with other children augured well for success in placement. Children who had siblings or other foster children with them did better; foster parents' own children, if young or close in age, were a risk factor (confirming the findings of Trasler and Parker). Foster mothers older than 40 years appeared to do better (also a finding of Trasler); experienced foster parents did much better, as did those who had preparation or training. In short-term and intermediate placements the findings were similar, although the breakdown rate was lower. In intermediate placement it appeared that better preparation and more social work contact were associated with stability; a longer care career and separation from siblings were associated with breakdown.

The authors also carried out an intensive study of ten cases from which they identify the following themes: the complexity of the breakdown process; the importance of negotiation before breakdown and of timely inputs from the social worker; the existence of contrasting expectations between carers and social workers; carers' isolation from social work support; the exclusion of natural parents from placements; poor coordination of services, and resource difficulties.

Berridge and Cleaver's is an important study with implications for contemporary practice. Many of its conclusions are of course based on associations between variables, and sometimes causal relationships are assumed without sufficient justification. In addition because the focus is on 'breakdown' the research tends to exclude planned or administrative moves which are also an important form of instability.

Factors in placement breakdown

In 1991 Joan Fratter, Jane Rowe, David Sapsford and June Thoburn published the results of a major study of more than 1000 permanent placements of children by voluntary agencies over a ten-year period. In looking at placement breakdown they concluded that the overwhelming majority of disruptions happen in the first two years and that the rate of disruption increases steadily with age at placement. Placement with siblings appeared to be a protective factor, as did family contact.

The authors used a sophisticated statistical technique known as *logit analysis* to isolate the effect of different factors on stability of placement, and they identified nine risk factors that were clearly associated with breakdown of placement:

● being older at placement

● being of mixed parentage

● being described as institutionalised

● having a history of deprivation or abuse

● being described as having behavioural difficulties

● being described as having emotional problems

● needing contact with siblings or relatives placed elsewhere but not parents

- having additional special needs or problems other than those listed.

Age at placement and the presence of emotional problems were the factors most strongly predictive of failure.

One of Fratter and her colleagues' principal conclusions from their study was that 'the task of identifying factors associated with successful outcomes in permanent placement is a difficult one.... different variables are associated with different outcomes for different groups of children' (p. 56). They suggest that future research would do well to concentrate on particular groups of children, since the implications for practice are likely to be different in different cases.

Permanent family placement in Newcastle

Joy Holloway made a retrospective study of all planned permanent placements made in Newcastle from 1986 to 1990 (Holloway, 1997b). By the time she collected her data in 1994, 20% of the placements had 'disrupted'. Like other researchers, Holloway found that disruption was strongly associated with the child's age at the time of placement. She also found that rates varied for different placement types, with adoption and fostering 'with a view to' adoption being apparently more successful than long-term foster placement in ensuring stability over the three to eight years preceding the study. However, differences in placement type were very closely associated with differences in age at placement, and when age was controlled for the association with placement type disappeared. (Children over seven were almost without exception placed as foster children. Below that age the majority were placed for adoption, and most of the rest were fostered with a view to adoption; while below one year all but one were placed for adoption.) In this study disruption was not associated with special needs, the sex of the child, a history of previous disruption, or being placed with siblings. Unlike Berridge and Cleaver (1987) Holloway found that 44% of children from disrupted placements returned to live with their birth families.

Holloway also looked at foster and adoptive mothers' evaluations of the success of permanent placement (Holloway, 1997a). She found that more than 90% of placements made when children were under seven were rated as 'very successful' by the mothers, but that only 31% of placements made after that age were so rated. However, a third of the adoptive and foster mothers had experienced major difficulties in the placement and six carers said that more medical/psychiatric input would have prevented breakdown. This is also one of the findings from Sonia Jackson's current study of the health of looked after children.

Institutional instability

A great deal of the research we have reviewed is concerned with the factors that cause placements to 'break down' or 'disrupt': often factors to do with characteristics of children or their families or with the skills of the carers and the support available to them. It would be easy to focus on these factors, and perhaps to assume that agencies are doing their best in difficult circumstances and that all that is needed to improve stability is more effective practice. This would be to ignore all the many ways in which the system produces instability for children. It is quite clear from the evidence that some children are being subjected to almost continuous change in their living arrangements for which there is no possible justification and which is utterly destructive of their well-being, development and chances of forming relationships. Apart from the failures of policy and management which produce the horrific figures quoted above there are two kinds of institutional instability and discontinuity to which we would like to draw attention.

The first – and we are indebted for this observation to members of our advisory group – is the built-in instability of many placements which officially count as stable, especially in residential establishments. Because of shift patterns, staff turnover, and the use of agency and contract staff, a child may be faced with different carers every day (or even before and after school); and a child who remains in an establishment for a long time can easily find that s/he has been there longer than most of the care staff. In both residential and other placements children may also suffer from changes of social worker or periods without a social worker, which again may mean that although they may appear in the records as having a stable placement, they are not receiving consistent care and oversight.

The second kind of institutional instability is that produced by the organisation of social work agencies. Policies and budgets may be drawn up in ways that do not promote stability or that actively promote instability – by producing moves dictated by financial considerations, closures of establishments, welfare policies that encourage agencies to propel young people into early and false 'independence'. Organisations themselves suffer disruption and upheaval, and staff who are uncertain about their own future may be ill-placed to give children a sense of security.

The organisation Voice for the Child in Care (VCC), which provides advocacy services for children and young people who are looked after, told us that 'we constantly have appeals for help from children who are about to be moved for financial reasons' (Gwen James, private communication). John Kemmis, VCC's Advocacy Officer, confirms that they frequently deal with children and young people who face moves which are clearly motivated by financial considerations, even though sometimes other reasons may be given. VCC's recent publication *Shout to be Heard*, which is based on children and young people's own stories, gives some vivid examples (VCC, 1998).

Local government reorganisation into smaller areas has reduced the flexibility that the old larger authorities previously had, both in terms of the range of placements available to them and their ability to budget for more expensive placements from time to time. Private fostering agencies used in an emergency are more expensive than local authority placements, producing pressure for a further move. In addition, private residential establishments may be under-resourced, with poorly trained staff, so that young people who may have behavioural or emotional problems are repeatedly rejected as unmanageable.

Ian and Robby's Story

Ian and Robby, brothers aged ten and nine, were admitted to a children's home after their mother died, and then moved to a foster home. They told the story three years later:

> 'We felt scared and angry when we were moved. But we settled in and we expected to stay here until we grew up. Our care plan said that we would stay in our foster home "with a view to permanency". We planted a tree in a local cemetery in memory of our mother.' Then came 'THE BOMBSHELL: Our social worker told our foster carers about Social Services' plan to move us. He said he didn't agree with the plan but that he was being told he had to move us. He did explain that we had rights. This bombshell fell and it was a very difficult time.'

Ian and Robby were helped by an advocate from VCC, who facilitated a financial agreement between Social Services and the fostering agency which enabled them to stay in their placement.

from Voice for the Child in Care (1998)

Key points from Chapter 4

- Moving is a stressful experience for anyone, especially for those, like most looked after children, who feel they have little control over the process.

- Any separation from an attachment figure is potentially harmful, and the cumulative effect of a series of upheavals and disruptions is extremely damaging to children.

- Research consistently points to a high level of instability and change for the majority of children in the care system when compared to children who remain with their own families.

- Most looked after children have to deal with several changes of placement, and some endure a very large number.

- Factors associated with placement stability and breakdown include the child's age, the presence of other children and the child's behaviour – or adult perceptions of the child's behaviour.

- The pioneering studies of stability in foster care were those by Trasler, Parker and George. Many of their findings are consistent with more recent research.

- Berridge and Cleaver's study of foster home breakdown remains the most substantial one in recent years. Like the earlier studies, it tells us mainly about associative rather than causal relationships.

- The study by Fratter and colleagues also tells us a good deal about factors associated with stability and breakdown. The authors point out that such broad associations may apply differently to different groups of children.

- Much instability is produced by institutional factors, rather than by characteristics of children or their placements. However these have attracted much less attention from researchers.

CHAPTER 5 : STABILITY IN DIFFERENT SETTINGS

In this chapter we focus on stability in the sense that it is most commonly used, that is the duration of a placement for as long as it is needed. As we have already pointed out, this is not the same as continuity, which we consider in more detail in Chapter 6.

A placement may end in a number of different ways:

● the child returns to his or her family

● the child is placed for adoption

● the child is transferred to a new placement at her/his own request

● the placement is ended because the carer is no longer willing to look after the child

● the child is moved from a short term placement having outstayed the time allocated to it

● the child is transferred to a new placement for administrative reasons such as cost, a reorganization of services, the closure of a residential unit or a change in local authority policy

● a young person grows up and leaves care.

Any of these moves might initiate an improvement or a deterioration in the child's quality of life. Research does not usually tell us much about this, tending as it does to concentrate on relatively simple matters such as continuance or 'breakdown' and treating placement moves planned by professionals as unproblematic. Looked at from the child's point of view the cause of the move is irrelevant: all moves are likely to mean disruption of their daily lives and relationships, an experience of loss and change, which if not well handled may threaten the success of the new placement. A placement move which is often seen as the solution to a problem may set off a whole series of new problems.

Not all moves are bad: some placement endings represent desirable outcomes, for example returning to one's own family after being looked after away from home, a successful adoption, leaving care at 18 to go on to college. Other moves are clearly not in the child's interests and would not occur if stability were given higher priority in management and social work planning. It is usually possible to find some justification for a proposed change of placement, perhaps as part of a plan introduced by a new social worker, but viewed in the context of the child's overall care career change may be damaging in itself. Research by the Looking After Children team found that many social workers seriously underestimated the number of moves that children had experienced (Ward, 1995). In Chapter 4 we considered the evidence on the effect on children's development of repeated breaking of attachments and changes of environment.

Contrary to the common view, changes of placement are as likely to be associated with service factors as with the child's characteristics, background or behaviour. This is often disguised by the tendency of researchers to take the adult perspective. So, for example, the ending of a foster placement is rarely described as 'rejection by foster carers' but by the neutral term 'breakdown', as if this were an act of God rather than a willed decision by some person or persons.

We have already reviewed the evidence that the care system in Britain is characterised by extreme instability, with a high proportion of children experiencing multiple moves while being looked after by local authorities. In this chapter we look at the relative success of different types of placement or substitute care in creating stability of living conditions for children whose birth parents have difficulty in looking after them to what society considers a reasonable standard.

Social services intervention in families is ranged along a continuum, from providing support for parenting at one end, to removing children permanently from their birth families and placing them for adoption at the other. In between are a variety of possible forms of provision; to some extent the divisions between them are artificial, since children and young people move between them, sometimes repeatedly. It is also hard to compare different types of placement because the criteria that one might use to define stability are not always the same. For example is the significant factor geographical location – the physical surroundings – or the identity of the primary carer? A child living in a residential home over an extended period will almost certainly experience many changes of care staff, key workers and social workers and fellow-residents. On the other hand he or she can continue to attend the same school, walk around the same streets, socialise with the same non-care friends, take part in the same leisure activities. A child in long-term foster care might move house with the foster family and have to change schools, adjust to a new neighbourhood, and develop a whole new network of friends. None of these changes counts as a change of placement, but their cumulative effect on the child should not be ignored.

The majority of research studies do not provide us with any information on these important details which have such a direct bearing on continuity in children's lives. On the whole research has been most concerned with the question of placement breakdown, or unplanned endings, and not with the impact on the child's life of moving from one location or set of carers to another. Even on the question of stability as opposed to continuity the evidence is far from adequate. For example, few reports of research tell us anything about the subsequent careers of children whose placement broke down. The commonly used distinction between planned and unplanned moves also leaves many questions unanswered. When a children's home is closed for administrative or financial reasons the transfer of the girls and boys who live there to another unit or to foster homes may be planned but it is likely to be no less disruptive of their education, relationship with carers and friendship networks than any other change of placement. With the rapid contraction of the residential child care sector through the 1980s and '90s some young people faced this kind of upheaval in their lives several times over, rather like the experience of 'serial redundancy'.

For these reasons it is not always very meaningful to compare one type of placement with another, and other factors, such as the legislative framework within which children's services operate or the policy of the local authority, may have much more influence on the stability of children's living arrangements. It is important to bear this in mind when considering evidence from research in other countries, particularly as most of it comes from the United States where the care population, legal background and financial provisions are very different from our own.

The continuum of care

Placement at home

Ever since the Children Act 1948 it has been recognised that it is generally best for children to grow up in their own families. This view was strongly reinforced by the Children Act 1989 and the number of children placed away from home has almost halved over the past fifty years. The figures for looked after children include around 10 per cent living at home, either having been returned to their parents after a period in local authority accommodation or remaining at home under supervision.

In the United States, where the attempt to combat child abuse sucked huge numbers of children, especially from African-American, Hispanic and mixed parentage families, into out-of-home care, a strong counter-movement developed advocating

- *family preservation* – keeping children at home by providing intensive services to their parents

- and *reunification* – making energetic attempts to return children to their families from placement instead of allowing them to 'drift' in care.

This American version of 'permanency planning', with which the name of Anthony Maluccio is particularly associated (Maluccio et al., 1986) has echoes in the Children Act 1989. Over the last decade it has generated a large number of special projects in the United States which have been formally evaluated. The findings have generally been interpreted as positive in that they show that resources invested in family preservation or reunification (more usually called family support and rehabilitation in the British literature), can pay dividends, although it has to be acknowledged that many such interventions are unsuccessful or of dubious advantage to the children concerned, as we discuss later.

In Britain the research focusing on placement at home mostly reflects the position before the implementation of the Children Act in 1991. Elaine Farmer and Roy Parker (1991) looked at what happened to children 'home on trial', having been taken into care either as a result of abuse or neglect or to control their behaviour. They called the first group, mostly young children, 'protected' and the older group 'disaffected'. Although they were rather pessimistic about the quality of care that the children experienced back home, noting the reluctance of social workers to terminate a home-on-trial placement even when conditions were clearly unsatisfactory, overall they judged 44 per cent of these placements to be positive and 35 per cent to be adequate. Even so, 38 per cent of 'protected' placements broke down and half of those in the 'disaffected' group, sometimes after two years or more. Some children were subjected to repeated unsuccessful attempts to return them home, and the authors note that the rate of positive outcomes fell sharply even between one and two placements. Children who were functioning fairly adequately at the start of their care careers could become increasingly disturbed with each successive change of placement (p.41), as would be predicted from the literature on attachment and loss (Chapter 4). Having spent longer in care was also associated with less successful outcomes. The care careers of adolescents were particularly unstable. They often stayed with a succession of friends or other family members, though a high proportion eventually returned to live with a parent.

John Triseliotis and colleagues noted a similar phenomenon when they tracked teenagers looked after and supervised by social work departments in Scotland over a one year period (Triseliotis, Borland, Hill and Lambert, 1995). They comment on the extent to which troubled adolescents move around of their own accord, or as a result of being thrown out by exasperated friends and relatives. However, three quarters of their research group were back living with their parents at the end of the year. The conclusion was that on balance living with parents provided a better chance of stability than other forms of placement. However, it should also be noted that return to parents does not necessarily mean continuity with a child's previous life. Bullock et al. (1993) point out how often children and young people leaving care return to a household with an entirely different composition from the one they left: partners leave and others appear, sometimes with children of their own; babies are born; older siblings leave home; living arrangements change.

Fostering with relatives

The Children Act 1989 for the first time gave official recognition to the valuable role played by the extended family in many children's lives. Sending children to stay with relatives has always been an accepted way for parents to cope with temporary difficulties, and most families would do this in preference to involving social services. Problems arise when care is likely to be needed for a long period and people are having to manage on low incomes. Formally designating a grandmother or aunt as a foster carer allows the local authority to pay a fostering allowance and sometimes provides access to other forms of support. There is a growing body of research on foster placement with relatives, but it does not often distinguish between an official endorsement of an informal arrangement within the family where the purpose is mainly to provide additional financial help to the family, and the rather different situation when a social worker seeks out a relative who might be in a position to offer care and negotiates a placement. In the second case the relative does not necessarily live nearby and the child may not even know her very well. Although their common family background should provide an element of continuity, the experience from the child's point of view may not be so different from being placed in an unrelated foster home.

Foster care with relatives has grown very rapidly in the United States, where it is known as 'kinship care'. In some states the proportion of children in out-of-home care looked after by relatives has risen to 30 per cent, especially among black and Hispanic families. Care by relatives is less common in Britain: a survey in Hampshire found that only four per cent of children fostered in the county were with relatives (Gorin, 1997); although research by one of us in South Wales and the English borders found that, of looked after children between the ages of eight and twelve, more than 20% were being fostered with relatives (Thomas and O'Kane, forthcoming), suggesting that there may be wide regional variations in practice.

A study of 188 families by one of the leading American not-for-profit agencies, the Casey Family Program, found that placement with relatives did provide greater stability of placement than other forms of care. Children were doing better at school and showing fewer behaviour problems, and the relative foster parents were more likely to see maintaining contact with the biological family as an important part of their role (LeProhn and Pecora, 1994). There is some concern that lower standards of selection may be applied when the prospective foster carer is related to the child, but no evidence for this. Some studies suggest that less support is provided to relatives, whether because it is not felt to be needed or because active intervention by social workers is seen as more intrusive in these circumstances. If, as research clearly shows, placements with relatives are less likely to break down, the gain in stability may sometimes have to be weighed against quality of care and what practical alternatives are available. However it may be that with the same level of support as unrelated foster carers there could be gains both in stability and quality.

A number of other American studies confirm that placement with relatives is likely to lead to greater stability, though some suggest that it may reduce the chance of successful reunification with birth parents (Scannapieco, 1999). Mary Benedict and colleagues in a retrospective study in Baltimore compared 86 children placed with relatives and 128 placed with non-relatives. Those placed with relatives had fewer problems, better behaviour and fewer changes of placement in childhood, but outcomes in adulthood were similar for both groups (Benedict et al, 1996). Maryjane Link followed up 525 children placed in kinship foster care in New York State and found that the placements were very stable, a high proportion leading to adoption (Link, 1996). These studies are discussed further in Chapter 6.

Shared care with parents

The Children Act 1989 emphasised the provision of accommodation for children as a service to families in difficulty rather than as a punishment for inadequacy. The change in terminology from 'in care' to 'looked after' was designed to underline this principle, and the early 1990s saw a steep drop in compulsory admissions to care, though the figures have recently been rising again – 58% of children are now looked after under care orders (Department of Health, 1998c). Nevertheless one of the ideas behind the Children Act reforms was that of 'shared care' as put forward by the Short Report and the Review of Child Care Law (DHSS 1985b). 'Shared care' can mean a number of different things but the key point is that the plan for the child includes periods of accommodation and periods with the child's own family, on some kind of continuing basis. It is likely to be suitable for children whose parents are willing and able to care for them but for social or health reasons find it too stressful to do so continuously.

It may for instance mean the provision of regular and frequent 'respite' with the same foster carers, on the model of established respite care services for disabled children (Robinson, 1996; Aldgate, Bradley and Hawley, 1996). The important point about this form of care is that the service is negotiated directly between parents and foster carers or link families and the child always returns to the same foster family, in contrast to failed placements at home when a new placement will usually have to be arranged. When it works well and there is a good relationship between the two families, respite care can provide continuity for the child even though he or she is moving between two homes. There is wide variation between local authorities in the extent to which they offer this service or other forms of relief care, described in official statistics as 'a planned series of short term placements'. Some authorities provide this kind of shared care with parents for over a quarter of their looked after population while others hardly use it at all (Department of Health, 1998c).

Short term foster care

About half the children looked after by local authorities spend quite a short time away from home. 43 per cent of children looked after during 1997 were looked after for less than 8 weeks, and 27 per cent for less than 2 weeks. Many foster carers are approved specifically for short term placements, usually for a maximum of three months. It might seem a contradiction to discuss stability in relation to a foster placement that is only intended to last for such a brief period, but 'short term' covers a variety of different situations and the time limit may refer to the placement rather than the child's needs. When a child is very disturbed and difficult to manage even three months may exhaust the tolerance of the foster family. The experience of a child who is placed with one set of foster carers for the duration of a family crisis and then returns home is very different from one whose placement fails and who is then moved to two or three different families during the same period. There is also evidence that many placements initially designated short-term drift on for an indeterminate period. For example, the Hampshire study quoted above found that 89% of people approved as short-term or emergency carers had provided care for a child longer than planned. A dilemma for social workers is whether to allow this to happen when the child and foster carer have formed an attachment to each other but when there is sometimes pressure from managers to move the child on to release the short-term place.

Clive Sellick and June Thoburn in an earlier report in this series (Sellick and Thoburn, 1996) review the evidence on what they call task focused, temporary foster care, most of the British research referring to practice before the implementation of the 1989 Children Act. They do not refer to any studies which looked specifically at stability within the placement period. The 'tasks' are defined as providing family support, contributing to a successful return home, preparing the child for a long-term placement or providing a bridge to independence. One of the indicators of success is whether the placement lasted as long as needed but no evidence is provided on this question. The American studies focus almost entirely on reunification with the birth family.

Residential care

Residential care has been the subject of intensive research for many years, much of it negative, and has become an increasingly devalued form of provision. Only about 10 per cent of the care population, mostly older adolescents, are currently looked after in community homes, about the same number as are placed at home with parents, and this figure has fallen steadily for the last ten years. Research on residential care highlights the tension between stability and quality of care, since we know that in the past children spent long periods of time, sometimes the whole of their childhood, in children's homes which were at best unstimulating and often uncaring, and at worst where they were subjected to physical, sexual and emotional abuse (Levy and Kahan, 1991;Utting, 1991, 1997; Skinner, 1992 Kent, 1997). Although Utting is rather optimistic about much more stringent standards for selection and vetting of residential staff offering protection to children against the most serious forms of abuse, the picture of residential care presented by these five reports is a depressing one.

An overview commissioned by the Department of Health of twelve research studies relating to residential care highlights the variability within the sector and acknowledges the almost impossible task which many residential units are set (Department of Health, 1998b). The report comments that:

> residential homes need to be evaluated against three very different criteria. The first is their success in responding to short-term emergencies, the second is their capacity to provide a time for reflection and perhaps for treatment and the third is their success in providing a stable, homely environment in which young people can live for some time. A key issue concerns the degree to which these purposes can be handled successfully at the same home (p.79).

The evidence suggests that local authority homes are not very successful in meeting the second and third criteria. The dominant impression from all the studies reviewed is the extreme volatility of residential care as it currently exists.

A relatively new feature is the dramatic increase in the number of 'out of area' placements in private children's homes. Gibbs and Sinclair (1998) found that private homes had some marked advantages as well as disadvantages by comparison with local authority residential units. The

50

researchers described them as 'more like the residential homes of the past'. Staff were more therapeutically oriented, less concerned with keeping order, and more satisfied with their work. Their greater distance from the young people's homes and the inclusion of education on the premises made it easier for them to specify their aims and keep reasonable control of residents, thus tending to lead to greater stability – despite the fact that the children themselves were likely to be more disturbed and difficult than those in publicly-funded units.

A qualitative study by Dorothy Whitaker and colleagues at the University of York found instability a major problem for staff as well as residents. Key influences on the culture of the home were the rate of turnover of young people (very high in all studies), the proportion of emergency placements, the mix of young people and the stability of the staff group (Whitaker, Archer and Hicks, 1998).

These are only the latest in a long line of generally negative research findings, which together with the high cost of children's homes and the pressure to make financial savings led to a steady reduction in residential care provision throughout the 1990s. The first local authority to close all its homes was Warwickshire, a process that was closely monitored and the outcomes reported in the book *Closing Children's Homes* by David Cliffe with David Berridge (1991). Not a great deal of attention is given to the effect of this policy on the children. From an administrative point of view it was considered a success; contrary to predictions it was not necessary to place large numbers of children outside the county and most were transferred to foster homes. Cliffe and Berridge note, however, that there was little choice of foster placements, which limited the scope for choosing a family to meet the needs of a particular child. This is identified by all studies as a significant factor in foster home breakdown and is a continuing problem within the care system.

Although few other authorities followed the example of Warwickshire, almost all pursued a policy of closing homes and reducing their size, placing most younger children in foster care and strongly favouring family over residential placement. The Skinner Report on residential care in Scotland (1992) made a strong recommendation that all children under 12 should be in foster home care unless there were compelling reasons to the contrary. The proportion of children in foster placements rose steadily between 1987 and 1995, levelling off around 65 per cent, and the numbers in local authority community homes have fallen from 13,200 to 5,200. The destabilizing effect on the whole residential care sector is well described in David Berridge and Isabelle Brodie's book, *Children's Homes Revisited* (1998). Of the 20 homes studied by Berridge in 1985 only four were still open ten years later, and two of those were on the point of closure.

It hardly makes sense any longer to talk about stability in residential care because it is not designed to provide stability. Despite all attempts to extol the benefits of group living for some children in some circumstances, most social workers persist in treating residential care as a last resort for young people who have been unable to settle in foster homes or as a temporary refuge for sibling groups or children who need short term accommodation in an emergency until a suitable foster home becomes available. Children in residential units (it is significant that the term 'children's home' is falling out of use) are usually waiting for a foster placement and are not encouraged to put down roots where they are living. When, most unusually, Swansea Social Services Department opened a new, purpose-built home, it was only designed for stays of up to three months, though in practice many children stay longer.

The development in Swansea is one of a number in the UK that have attempted to improve the reputation and status of residential child care. The generally low value placed on residential care probably contributes to its instability and so justifies the poor opinion in which it is held by social workers. With so little accommodation available in most areas, emergency admissions are made without regard to the impact on existing residents or the composition of the group. Many residential units are in a state of constant turmoil, and it is not surprising that children and young people who are already disturbed behave in ways that add to the problems of staff and make them very unpopular in the surrounding community. The response is to move them on, either to other homes where the same problems recur, or, too often, to secure accommodation. If they are over sixteen they may be turned out to live in flats or bedsits in what is euphemistically called 'independent living', often without regard to their possession of the complex skills required. We discuss this issue in more detail below, and it is the subject of another report in this series, *What Works in Leaving Care?* by Mike Stein (1997).

However, it may be the way that residential child care is currently used in Britain, and not the fact of group living, that is responsible for its low reputation and poor outcomes. There is good evidence from other countries that high quality residential care can work to create stability and a good quality of life for children not able to live at home. It is also worth noting that residential schools, where children are expected to stay for several years at a time, have a much better record of keeping their pupils and improving their behaviour and attainments. Triseliotis et al. in their study of teenagers (1995) found that of placements planned to last for a whole year over 60% of residential school placements did so, compared with two out of nine residential home placements and three out of twelve foster placements. On the other hand, the reluctance of social workers to use residential care is illustrated by the fact that only one of eight moves to a residential unit was planned (compared with nearly two thirds of moves out of care, either to return home or to independent living).

The most impressive evidence that residential care for children can work, both in creating stability and in leading to satisfactory development and outcomes, comes from the longitudinal study carried out by Anita and Eugene Weiner in Israel (Weiner and Weiner, 1990). Paradoxically, the title of their report is *Expanding the Options in Child Placement*, and the book proposes raising the status of family foster care, usually regarded as an inferior form of placement in Israel. The Weiners were able to follow a group of 268 infants placed in children's homes throughout their childhood and into young adulthood. The children did not appear to suffer any of the effects of institutionalisation reported in so many other studies and almost all made an excellent adjustment to adult life. During a lecture tour of Israel undertaken in 1995 Sonia Jackson was able to visit a number of these homes, which were all different but had some common characteristics. It was evident that they had changed over the years and were constantly looking for ways to improve the children's experience, for example by breaking up the larger institutions into small living groups with their own quarters. In some ways their practice might still seem quite old-fashioned to a British visitor. What they had succeeded in doing was creating a stable living experience for the children in which they could confidently expect to be in the same place with the same carers for most if not all of their childhood. Most of the children stayed in their group homes until they reached the age to do their army service. Similarly the staff expected to remain in the same jobs for long periods of time and had formed close, loving relationships with the children. The majority were resident, not working shift systems but constantly available to the children. A further contrast with the British residential care system was the strong emphasis placed on education, both in school and in the homes. The idea of children being out of school or receiving no education seemed to be unthinkable.

Residential education is deeply rooted in Jewish and Israeli culture, and the extent to which the acknowledged success of residential care in Israel can be attributed to historical and cultural factors is discussed by several authors in a special issue of the journal *Residential Treatment for Children and Youth* (Beker and Magnuson, 1996). Most of the authors are American and draw out the differences between the facilitating, identity-enhancing regimes of Israeli residential homes and schools and the corresponding institutions in the United States, which are either punitive or therapeutic in orientation. In Israel, and to a lesser extent in continental Europe the task is defined as residential education, the fostering of normal development and the creation of a harmonious and stimulating living environment. US programs focus on behaviour management and containment, even when they are called 'treatment centres'. Allowing for the halo effect and being shown as a visitor the best of what a country has to offer, the contrast is still extreme, and one is left with an uncomfortable feeling that the British residential system has far more in common with the American model, failing to learn from more successful approaches in other European countries (Colton, Hellinckx, Ghesquiere and Williams, 1995).

Specialist foster care

An important alternative to residential care in recent decades has been the development of various kinds of specialist foster care, especially for adolescents or for children with emotional and behavioural difficulties. Although the cost of such placements can be very high we have not been able to find any research studies which compare 'traditional' and specialist or 'treatment' foster care using consistent definitions of success, and very few in the UK have been evaluated in any systematic way. The exception is the Kent Family Placement Scheme (now Pro-Teen), which was the original model for many of the others and is described in more detail in Chapter 7 (Hazel and Fenyo, 1993).

The typical features of such schemes are

- carers are paid an enhanced allowance or a professional fee

- additional training and support are provided

- there may be a different contractual basis, in that carers undertake to take certain placements for fixed lengths of time.

Such schemes can be effective in providing good and stable care for children and young people who otherwise might suffer a series of failed foster placements or remain in residential care. Although placements of this kind are not in most cases intended to provide *permanence* as it is normally understood, we have already seen how *stability* can also be important in a short or intermediate timescale, and a settled period before leaving care can be extremely important for a young person who has already suffered from disruption or upheaval. Celia Downes' work has shown how relevant are the concepts of attachment theory in this type of placement, in particular in relation to the process of transition from one setting to another (Downes, 1992).

However, it must be remembered that attachment processes do not necessarily work in the same way for adolescents entering placements as they do for younger children. Sandra Butler and Marian Charles at the University of Nottingham studied specialist foster care for teenagers in an attempt to understand some of the 'dynamics of disruption'. As part of a wider study of foster care services, they interviewed a small self-selected sample of carers and young people whose placements had broken down, in order to discover what kind of things might have gone wrong. Using this retrospective information, the authors found a marked conflict in expectations between carers and young people at the time of placement. Carers in general appeared to expect:

● that young people would become attached to their new families

● that they would be grateful for the opportunities they were offered

● and that they would change their lifestyle and behaviour.

The young people in contrast expected that there would be considerable difficulties associated with living in a different family. Perhaps because of their own negative experiences of family life, for them going into foster care was, in the words of one young man, 'a bit dodgy'. Many of their comments indicated suspicion and mistrust of the carers' motives for having them in their homes. On one reading, the young people had much more realistic expectations of the difficulties inherent in the enterprise. Butler and Charles ask why carers had such apparently naive expectations despite the training and preparation which they had received. They suggest that more emphasis on *difference* in preparation and training programmes might help carers to be more realistic, more accommodating and accepting of young people's backgrounds and personalities (Butler and Charles, 1998).

While there is considerable evidence of the success of specialist or treatment foster care from the American research, it is very difficult, as Berridge (1996) has pointed out, to disentangle all the features which distinguish it from 'traditional' fostering and identify which are the key factors. Is it the higher fees, the tendency of carers to come from a different class background and be better educated, improved training and support, or the fact that they are more likely to be treated by social workers as colleagues and less as clients?

Long-term foster care

Much of the research into stability has focused on long-term foster care, as we saw in the previous chapter. It is not necessary to repeat here the research findings that we have already quoted. It is clear that there are a number of factors that are highly predictive of breakdown in placements that were intended to be permanent, of which the most significant are the age of the child and the extent to which the carers find his or her behaviour difficult to deal with. What is surely required is a greater readiness to use these factors to predict the placements that will need greater support, and to plan for that support to be available from the outset. One further element which is very little discussed in the literature on breakdown is the degree of commitment by the foster carers, and this may indeed be the decisive factor.

There is debate about whether foster care can offer as secure a placement as adoption, with strongly held positions and some conflicting research findings. In our view the overwhelming weight of evidence is on the side of adoption offering the best chance of real permanence for children who cannot return to their families, especially if it can happen when the child is young. However, there will always be cases where a foster placement is the only realistic option, for example for older adolescents and where the child objects to the idea of adoption. Research suggests that there are things that can be done to give the placement a greater sense of permanence, for instance, by allowing long-term carers greater autonomy. In this connection it is unfortunate that so little use has been made of residence orders in foster care.

Adoption

Adoption is a very wide subject, but here we are mainly concerned with the evidence on how far placement for adoption can create stability for children already in the care system, or who would need to be looked after by local authorities if they were not placed for adoption.

Although adoption continues to be a legal procedure in which all rights and responsibilities for a child are transferred from the birth parents to the adoptive parent(s), the institution of adoption has undergone radical change in the last thirty years. First, as the supply of babies diminished with better contraception, the legalisation of abortion and more liberal attitudes towards single motherhood and births outside marriage, adoption became a possibility for older children and those with disabilities. Second, the all-or-nothing character of adoption has begun to change with increasing acceptance of the idea of 'open' adoption in which some degree of contact, or at least communication, between the new family and the family of origin is seen as desirable. There seems to be a growing consensus that continuing contact with birth parents is a good thing, both in fostering and adoption. At present this is only weakly supported by research. A critical review by David Quinton and colleagues (Quinton, Rushton, Dance and Mayes, 1997) concludes that the majority of studies pointing in that direction are flawed. The evidence is unclear either way: contact does not appear, as was once thought, to undermine placements, but neither can it be said, on the present evidence, significantly to enhance stability.

Expanding the categories of children seen as potentially adoptable meant that the previous rationing system excluding many would-be adopters became less necessary. The emphasis shifted from finding a 'perfect' child to meet the desire of a childless couple to become parents to finding a permanent home for any child who needed one. Adoption subsidies or allowances are an important aspect of the more child-centred view of adoption and may make it possible, for example, for families to adopt foster children when they would otherwise be prevented for financial reasons.

The character of adoption continues to change and if, as in the past, the main direction of change is from the United States to Britain, we may see a reaction against the tight regulation and bureaucratic procedures which appear to be obstacles to greater use of adoption as a form of alternative care. Independent adoptions, negotiated between birth and adoptive parents with a lawyer, doctor or private agency acting as intermediary, are increasingly common in America, though illegal in this country. Instead of prospective adopters choosing a child from a list or album of photographs or relying on an agency to inform them that a child is available, the birth parent(s) choose the people they would like to bring up their child. In the case of baby adoptions the new parents may even live with an expectant mother during the final stages of the pregnancy and be present at the birth. This is a very different experience for the mother from handing over a child to the representative of an agency and makes continuing exchange of information and news a less contrived or externally imposed activity (Fein, 1998). Independent adoptive placements are legal in all but six US states though there has to be a study of the adoptive home by a licensed agency before the adoption is allowed.

However, in both Britain and America infant adoptions are in a minority and most children available for adoption come through the public care system. As child welfare services increasingly emphasise reunification of birth families (Marsh and Triseliotis, 1993) children eventually released for adoption come from more disturbed homes and more difficult experiences, probably in a series of placements, compounding their initial problems.

The number of looked after children placed for adoption in Britain is extremely small and continued to decline steadily between 1992 and 1997. The number of adoption orders granted went down from 2,500 in 1993 to under 2000 in 1996. A study by Gilles Ivaldi for BAAF from the records of 1,507 children adopted in 1996 revealed long delays in finding placements and between placement and adoption. Just over half of the children had entered care under the age of 1 year, but even infants voluntarily relinquished for adoption had to wait on average until they were 13 months before the adoption order was granted. Older children waited longest: those admitted to care aged 5 years or older waited on average another five years for adoption. Over a third of the children experienced three or more placements before adoption, and there were wide variations between authorities, ranging from 0 to 9 per cent of children looked after.

The significance of this study becomes apparent when it is viewed alongside the very strong evidence that success or failure in adoption is closely related to the age of the child at placement. This does not mean that late adoption cannot be successful but the chances of success are much reduced. Triseliotis, Shireman and Hundleby (1997) provide a very comprehensive review of the evidence on this point. Once it becomes clear that the birth parents will not be able to provide a home for the child every year of delay in placing him or her for adoption makes a successful placement less likely.

Almost every aspect of adoption has been exhaustively researched, and it is not always easy to compare studies because definitions of 'success' vary so widely. The adoption of a baby following one transitional foster placement is a very different phenomenon from the adoption of a 15-year-old boy who has moved between ten different residential and foster homes. It is reasonable to measure success for early-placed children against outcomes for the general population, but for later adoptions the comparison should probably be with children who remain in public care. A further problem in evaluating research studies is intrinsic to the subject. Whatever indicators of success are used – stability, educational achievement, emotional health, social adjustment, subjective experience of child or adopters – they can really only be measured in retrospect, when the child has grown up. By then the world has changed so much that the results have only limited relevance to current policy and practice. The majority of prospective studies follow children for at most three to five years and although most failed adoptions break down in the first year (Triseliotis et al, 1997), it cannot be assumed that young children whose adoptive placements last for five years will necessarily remain in the same home to adulthood.

Another problem is that age and other factors are conflated. 'Older' and 'special needs' are often used interchangeably, but age is an objective fact whereas 'special needs' is a euphemism covering a wide variety of circumstances with different implications for the viability of adoption. Barbara Tizard's important study, *Adoption: A second chance* (Tizard, 1977), showed that, contrary to previous assumptions, older children adopted from institutions could form secure attachments to their new parents if given the opportunity. Some children have the capacity to recover from the most adverse early experiences (Haggerty et al, 1994). Others who have been seriously abused or neglected continue to show extreme behavioural and emotional disturbance even after years of loving care, and this can severely test the placement, particularly in adolescence (Cairns, 1999). 'Special needs' is also used to mean 'hard-to-place', that is, unattractive to potential adopters because of disability, physical appearance, or membership of a less-valued ethnic group, but once the placement has been made these characteristics, unlike behavioural problems, do not seem to carry any greater risk of disruption.

Author(s)	Date	Short title	Country	R
Parker	1966	*Decisions in Child Care*	England	S
Stein, Gambrill and Wiltse	1978	*Achieving Continuity of Care*	USA	R
Berridge and Cleaver	1987	*Foster Home Breakdown*	England	Fi ca
Rowe et al	1989	*Child Care Now*	England	S
Fratter et al	1991	*Permanent Family Placement*	England	S
Triseliotis et al	1995	*Teenagers and Social Work Services*	England & Scotland	S
Ward (ed.)	1995	*Looking After Children: research into action*	England	S
Staff and Fein	1995	*Stability and change*	USA	S
Link	1996	*Permanency outcomes in kinship care*	USA	L
Palmer	1996	*Placement stability in foster care*	Canada	Pr
Tam and Ho	1996	*Prospect of children returning to their parents*	Hong Kong	S
McAuley	1996	*Children in Long Term Foster Care*	Northern Ireland	Pr
Quinton et al	1997	*Contact between children in placement and birth parents*	Cross-national	R
Stein	1997	*What Works in Leaving Care?*	UK	R
Triseliotis et al	1997	*Adoption*	Cross-national	R
Berridge and Brodie	1998	*Children's Homes Revisited*	England	Q

type	No. of subjects	Key finding
	209	Presence of own children close in age to foster child is predictive of breakdown
	428	Behavioural work with parents increases return; long-term foster care leads to instability
es	372	Placement factors produce more breakdowns than child factors
	2010 (4940 placements)	'Nearly half of all placements end with a move to another in-care placement'
	1000+	Most disruptions in first 2 years; placement with siblings a protective factor
	116	Staying at home offers best stability; residential schools more stable than care homes
	204 looked after; 379 in community	Discontinuity reduced by systematic tracking linked to action
	244 (540 placements)	Most social work time spent on arranging multiple placements for small number of children
inal study	525	Kinship placements more stable
ve study	184	'Inclusive practice' leads to greater stability
	877	Return more likely when parents involved in day-to-day care
ve study	19	Impact on children of change of school and loss of contact with friends on changing placement
f research	18 studies	Evidence of positive or negative effects of contact too weak for practice guidance
review	n.a.	Success of leaving care schemes depends on quality and continuity of previous care
review	n.a.	Adoption the most stable form of placement
e survey	12 homes	Residential sector chronically unstable; most teenagers stay a short time and move often

A striking example of the way adoption can transform such children's life chances is provided by the Barnardo's longitudinal study of 12 children with Down's Syndrome adopted by families in North East England (Hughes, Mason and Selman, 1998). These children, now aged 12 to 16, might otherwise have spent their lives in institutions, and the idea that they might be adopted was still considered innovative at the time the first children in the study were placed. At the third stage follow-up, as the children approached school-leaving age, all the children are still with their original adoptive parents and making good progress. The researchers, from the University of Newcastle, conclude:

> The adoption of the child with Down's Syndrome has been demonstrated to be a potentially rewarding and positive experience for the host family, and a nourishing and valuable source of security and happiness for the child. None of the families had any regrets about their experiences and all of the children appeared to be content and flourishing.

Adoptive families where the child was placed in infancy appear to be no less stable than natural families. For 'special needs' children placed under the age of 10 the success rate is around 90%. When children are placed later the success rate drops to about 75%, and continues to fall the later the placement is made. The findings for younger children are fairly consistent, with both British and American studies reporting a disruption rate of about 10 per cent, increasing sharply in early adolescence, but the findings on children placed at over 14 years vary widely between 26% (Barth and Berry, 1988) and 40–50% Thoburn and Rowe, 1988).

An important study in progress is the longitudinal research by Michael Rutter and his colleagues on Romanian children adopted by British families following the most extreme experience of early privation (Rutter et al., 1998). Conditions in the 'hospitals' or 'orphanages' from which the children came are described as varying 'from poor to appalling'. For example washing often consisted of being hosed down with cold water. Nevertheless, the first report shows that children placed at less than six months had caught up with their age group almost completely by the time they were four, and even those adopted later (up to two years) improved dramatically on all measures. Most significant for our purposes, despite the children's gross retardation and often extremely challenging behaviour, the breakdown rate after four years was only 1.8%. Inter-country adoption is such a demanding process that probably only the most determined persist with it, and it may be that the stability of these placements, in the most difficult circumstances, reflects above all the commitment of the parents.

It is sometimes suggested that because some studies have found failure rates for children placed in adolescence not much different from disruptions of long-term foster placements that there is no advantage in adoption, and that the experience of rejection may be even more devastating for the child because of the expectation of permanence. What we cannot know is how many, especially those who had already spent many years in care, might have been successfully adopted had they been placed at an earlier age. Moreover, the longer-term outlook for a child who is legally adopted is very different from the prospects of the foster child for whom local authority payments cease at 18 at the latest and whose carers have no further obligation towards him or her. Studies of careleavers who cannot return to their families paint an almost unrelieved picture of lonely, ill-prepared young people living on the margins of society at high risk of all kinds of social problems. Even those who have had a relatively good care experience face enormous difficulties in moving on without the background support most young people can take for granted (Stein, 1997; Broad, 1998). For the small minority who go on to further or higher education the practical and emotional obstacles are so great that only the most determined survive (Jackson and Martin, 1998). The abolition of maintenance grants and introduction of tuition fees is likely to make things even harder for them. Adoptive parents, by contrast, usually see supporting their child educationally as a high priority, even if it involves financial hardship for themselves. It is worth noting that there is provision for both fostering and adoption allowances to continue beyond 18 for young people in full time education but some local authorities are very reluctant to make such payments.

Discussion

This review of different types of substitute care underlines the weakness of the evidence on what works in creating stability. In all but a handful of studies information on stability is a by-product of the research and not its main focus. Comparing categories of care can be a misleading exercise, both because so many children move from one to another, and because the meaning of the category changes over time. What do today's small residential units with three or four children have in common with the sixty bed homes of the past? In the past foster parents were enjoined to treat foster children as if they were their own; now their job is usually to work towards the child's return home and avoid taking over the parental role. This must inevitably undermine their commitment to the child and their willingness to continue to care when the going gets tough and the rewards seem small. The conflict that the contradictory demands on foster parents can create was vividly illustrated by the much-publicised case of Jeff and Jennifer Bramley, who abducted their foster daughters and remained in hiding for four months when their application to adopt was opposed by the social services department.

What is clear is that removing children from home carries a high risk of launching them into a lifetime of chaos and confusion. In that sense the reluctance of local authorities to undertake the care of children unless it is unavoidable is well-founded. The best chance of stability for most children is to remain with one at least of their birth parents. If that is not possible, fostering with relatives is more likely to produce a stable placement than fostering with strangers. Residential education has the potential to offer greater stability than residential care, but the continuation of the placement may depend on fragile agreements between local authority departments and sometimes across different authorities. These are often time-limited and may lead to the placement ending for administrative or financial reasons. From the child's perspective this must be wrong, but the high cost of some residential school placements presents real problems for some of the new, smaller authorities.

There is more detailed evidence on adoption and its outcomes than on any other form of placement. It has generated a vast body of research in the United States and in Europe, particularly in relation to inter-racial and inter-country adoption (see Triseliotis, Sellick and Short, 1995, for a comprehensive review, Morgan, 1997 for a polemical statement of the case for adoption). Several important studies are due to report later this year, and an authoritative overview of research on adoption commissioned by the Department of Health is also in preparation. However, there is already plenty of evidence that adoption offers by far the best chance of stability for children who cannot live with their families. It is the only form of placement that guarantees the adopted child the same permanency and lifelong commitment that other children have in their family of birth, including practical and emotional support in adulthood.

In the face of this overwhelming body of evidence, it is reasonable to ask why many social workers continue to favour long-term fostering over adoption even when return to the birth family is not a possibility, and why some children freed for adoption wait five years for adoptive placements. June Thoburn (1990) argues that what is important is the sense of permanency that a family creates for the child, which in her study was not necessarily related to the legal status. However, Triseliotis and Russell (1984) found that adoption was strongly preferred by young people themselves, giving them a sense of security and belonging that they felt they lacked even in foster homes where they had lived for many years.

Key points from Chapter 5

- Changes of placement are as likely to be caused by service factors as by the child's characteristics. 'Placement breakdown' usually means rejection by foster carers.

- Remaining at home or returning quickly offers the best chance of stability and continuity for most children.

- Shared care with parents on the respite model can provide continuity and keep families together.

- Placement with relatives is the most stable form of foster care.

- Residential care can provide stability and continuity but seldom attempts to do so in this country.

- Specialist or professional foster care placements are less likely to end sooner than planned and may sometimes provide ongoing support into independence.

- For children who cannot live with parents or extended family, adoption at whatever age offers by far the best chance of long-term stability and relationship, but the success rate is closely related to age of placement.

CHAPTER 6 :
PROMOTING CONTINUITY

As we said in Chapter 2, we try to distinguish in this book between stability, by which we mean a child remaining in the same placement, and continuity, by which we mean the maintenance of stable networks of relationships, personal and cultural identity, education and health care.

It is important to make this distinction because stability does not necessarily imply continuity, and vice versa. A child may remain in the same placement and yet experience considerable *dis*continuity; or may move from place to place and yet have continuity in other aspects of his or her life. We need to ask whether continuity in relationships or in education, for instance, can compensate at least to some extent for a lack of stability in placement; and what should happen if choices have to be made between placement stability and other aspects of continuity.

In general it seems likely that stability and continuity will go together. For instance Catherine Shaw in her survey of children and young people for the Who Cares? Trust found that 'after the first six months in care, children who had been looked after in a single setting were markedly more positive and settled at school than those who had been moved around' (Shaw, 1998, p. 67). Louise Garnett in her study of care leavers for the National Children's Bureau found that of the three groups of leavers (teenage entrants, long-term stable, long-term unsettled), the 'long-term stable' did much better in education and employment (Garnett, 1992). Annick Dumaret's study of children's villages in France, where placements tended to be extremely stable, found that school achievement was better than for children in traditional foster care or with their own families, especially for children placed under the age of six (Dumaret, 1988). Berridge and Cleaver's classic study of foster home breakdown found that social networks were important in maintaining stability: contact with families, continuity of school, supportive relationships with other children, all augured well for maintaining the child in placement (Berridge and Cleaver, 1987).

On the other hand there is considerable research evidence that stability of placement can be combined with a lack of continuity or consistency in other aspects of a child's life. In recent years a body of research into the experience of children looked after has shown that even those with relatively stable placement histories may suffer crucial gaps in their education and health care and lack proper support and surveillance (Fletcher-Campbell, 1997, Borland et al., 1998, Jackson, 1994, Berridge, Brodie and Beckett, 1996). Frequent changes of social worker, inadequate record-keeping and failure to maintain links with birth families all lead to discontinuity with very adverse consequences for the children (Parker et al., 1991;Ward, 1995). The Dartington Social Research Unit's study, *Lost in Care* (Millham et al., 1986), showed how children in long-term care often lost touch with their families and might find themselves at sixteen alone in the world. Later research on children returning home from care found that families had often changed composition or moved house in their absence – aspects of discontinuity which must be extremely important to children, and if not adequately prepared for may threaten their successful reintegration into the family (Bullock et al., 1993).

Education is the aspect of children's lives where it is most vital to preserve continuity, in relationships with teachers and friends, attendance at lessons, keeping up with curriculum content, ensuring understanding of important elements of each subject. There is much evidence of the failure of social services to give any attention to these matters (Fletcher-Campbell and Hall, 1990). Moves in care nearly always involve changes of school, or such long and difficult journeys to avoid a transfer that the benefits of not changing are lost. Cliffe and Berridge (1991) in their study of closing children's homes, found that almost half the moves they noted involved either a school change or serious transport difficulties. Berridge and Cleaver (1987) noted that placements were more likely to break down when children had to move school as a result of a change, and Farmer and Parker (1991) found that half of the older children in their study had been in three or more placements, each involving a change of school, to which they partly attribute the poor attendance records of the young people after their return home. The relationship works both ways: doing well at school makes it more likely that the placement will be a success, and school problems are a significant cause of coming into care and of placement breakdown.

Borland et al (1998) point out the impact of frequent moves on school attainment, but add that this does not inevitably lead to educational failure. A minority of children do well at school despite typically unstable care careers, It is the emphasis on continuity of learning opportunities, which need to be highly individualised and subject related, that seems to make the difference. There should be an expectation that teachers will liaise with each other, which hardly ever happens now, and this will probably need to be mediated by the social worker. When foster carers give high priority to education they usually take the lead in trying to create some continuity between children's past and present school experience, but in the past this has not been seen as an important part of their role. What seems to be needed to avoid a deterioration in school performance as a result of placement moves is very detailed attention to exactly what the child has been doing in the previous school and will be doing in the new one, ensuring that they are not moved to different courses or lower groups as a result of the change. This is particularly essential for teenagers, who are most vulnerable to repeated changes during the years when they should be preparing for GCSE examinations. The loss of coursework during transitions and disruption of school attendance in the period coming up to exams are frequently reported by young people, and at least partly account for the fact that fewer than 3 per cent of those looked after achieve five GCSE passes at A-C grades compared with over 60% of the age group (Jackson and Martin, 1998).

Children's views on stability and instability

Most studies of children and young people's views on being in care have found distress at being moved from one placement to another, and frequently resentment at their lack of involvement in decisions about placement (see for instance Fletcher, 1993; Dolphin Project, 1993; Shaw, 1998).

Nigel Thomas and Claire O'Kane studied the participation of children aged 8–12 in decisions when they were looked after by local authorities (Thomas and O'Kane, 1998). They found that most children felt they had little say over what happened when they first came into care or accommodation, even if they had initiated the process themselves. Some children were subsequently involved in placement moves in which they felt involved and engaged, but many others experienced the process as alien and outside their control. Children and their carers spoke eloquently of their disturbance and distress at repeated moves, sometimes without apparent reason, explanation or warning. As one eight year old boy put it, 'The very first time I went, they didn't let me visit or anything, they just took me there. This time I visited, but I didn't really want to come here. They just made me come.'

The poor handling of moves and the lack of preparation or information given to children is a recurring theme in the literature. Rosalind Folman interviewed 91 children between 8 and 14 about their experience of going into care in Massachusetts. They described their overwhelming feelings of fear, bewilderment and abandonment, exacerbated by false reassurance from well-meaning caseworkers. One 10-year-old boy was told he would be going home the next day and commented: 'They do that so you'll stop crying. They shouldn't have lied. They should have told me'. However neglectful or even abusive their parents may have been, removal leads to fears of being totally abandoned, and for some children this was made even worse by separation from siblings. Their sense of helplessness made it difficult for the children to ask questions or to process information given to them. In most of the cases she studied Folman concluded that the failure of the system to validate children's perceptions and feelings by defensively denying the pain of separation confirmed the children's working models of adults as people who cannot be trusted and of themselves as unworthy of care. The way the placement process was handled undermined the children's ability to adapt to their loss and to develop new attachments (Folman, 1998).

Children's perspectives on long-term foster care

Colette McAuley carried out an intensive study of children during the first two years of their planned long-term placement, concentrating on their developing relationships with parents, carers and significant others (McAuley, 1996). She found that:

- 'A dominant theme emerging from the interviews with the children was that of the impact of the loss of contact with friends and significant others as a result of the move into the foster placement... sadness and resentment were expressed by the children about losing contact with their friends in their previous foster homes and schools. A considerable number of the children had been placed from residential homes and many indicated that they missed the other children there' (p. 156–7).

- Nearly all of the children had had to change school when they moved to their new placement, and many were sad and resentful at the loss of contact with friends and teachers. McAuley also points out that several of the children had changed schools for a similar reason previously and that their generally poor educational attainment should be seen in this context; she also notes that in most cases there was no alternative placement available.

- Most of the children were preoccupied with their birth parents, notwithstanding the fact that in most cases they had been abused by them. Their responses to questions indicated that they still identified mainly with their birth parents after two years in placement (although as early as the four-month stage their foster parents were the people to whom they said they would entrust their concerns).

- Most children were also concerned for their siblings, with whom they mostly had contact; 'often that contact was very important to these children and seemed to compensate for lack of contact with parents at times by maintaining a sense of family identity... they had travelled through troubled times together' (p. 158).

- 'Many of the children with established positive relationships with their birth parents felt that they did not have their permission to be fostered... the children's reaction was predominantly one of sadness' (p. 159). McAuley suggests that this raises questions about whether the parents had received counselling following the children's admission to care and an opportunity 'to express their feelings about the admission and to consider the important continuing role they could play in the lives of their children', and also about whether any direct work was carried out with the children. She concludes that 'there was little evidence that the children in this study had this preparation' (*ibid.*).

- The research also found that children whose placements went on to disrupt were assessed by their foster parents as having high levels of behaviour problems and low levels of social competence; although teachers' ratings for these children were not different than for those children who remained in placement. This suggests that foster carers' perceptions of children's behaviour may sometimes be as important as the behaviour itself.

Both Folman's and McAuley's studies remind us that the process of a child 'settling in' to a substitute family is a complex and delicate one and that skilled and sensitive social work may be needed in order to make it work.

Attempts to improve stability and continuity

Many attempts have been made to improve stability and continuity for children looked after away from home, by changing policy or practice.

Some of these developments were mentioned in the previous chapter. In this chapter we look more closely at some of the attempts which have been made to improve the service and outcomes for children and young people.

Family and Adolescent Support Services

John Brown (1998) reviewed the work of adolescent support services for the National Institute of Social Work. There are about 60 teams of this kind in England usually consisting of teams of 4–8 workers. All were created with the objective of reducing the rate of admission to looked after accommodation, targeting the 10–16 age range. They work intensively with each family for short periods (up to 3 months) with small caseloads of five to ten families, visiting each two or three times a week until the crisis which threatened to precipitate the young person into care abates.

The success rate is estimated at 80%–90%, in other words separation was avoided in nearly nine out of every ten cases. Feedback from families was positive, especially because they found the service less stigmatising than conventional social work and experienced the workers as geared to keeping the family together rather than assessing their competence as parents. This is line with the findings of the Alameda project (Stein et al, 1978). Several teams who employed educational liaison teachers as a means of reintegrating adolescents back into schools reported 'enormous benefits' particularly for inter-agency cooperation.

Some other features of the services which seemed to help them to achieve success in family preservation were having workers with a variety of experiences and backgrounds and using befrienders, mentors and volunteers alongside them. Making specific arrangements with leisure services to find ways of occupying the teenagers and getting them out of the family home also proved helpful.

The report suggests that lack of appropriate skills in assessment and communication with adolescents among social workers can lead to too hasty resort to (usually residential) accommodation whereas dedicated family and adolescent support services can successfully divert young people from residential care and are extremely cost-effective compared with providing accommodation. No reliable evaluation studies have yet been carried out but it is clear that if problems can be resolved without separation from the family the chances of the young person experiencing continuity and stability are very much higher than if they enter the care system. Brown comments that the local authorities have given a general social work task to experienced workers from other services and in effect created a new form of specialist and more intensive adolescent-focused social work. (Brown, 1998. See also 'Family and Adolescent Support Services: new social work crisis, support and assessment services for adolescents and their families.' A discussion paper for the National Institute for Social Work, April 1998.)

Reunification

One way to improve stability and continuity is to seek to return more children to their families of origin. Most research suggests that this becomes increasingly unlikely the longer the child remains away from home, and there may be questions about how far it is in the child's best interest, especially when it results in several unsuccessful attempts at reunification. It also tends to be extremely costly in resources. We have not found any schemes in this country which employ a well-defined form of intervention and systematic evaluation, but there have been many such studies in America related to the requirement in federal legislation that children removed from home as a result of abuse and neglect must have a plan for permanency.

Edith Fein and Ilene Staff report on an intensive family reunification programme provided for public welfare agencies in New England by the Casey Family Services Program (Fein and Staff, 1993). The authors cite research which indicates that 'two-thirds to three-quarters of the youngsters who enter foster care are reunified with their families in under two years' (p. 25). The Casey programme, however, works with families whose circumstances make reunification 'especially difficult' – in most cases single mothers living in poor housing and with serious financial difficulties, in many cases with serious problems of substance abuse and/or domestic violence.

Reunification is targeted to take place within six months after case acceptance, and worker involvement can continue for 18 months after reunification. Services are delivered by a two-person team – a social worker and a family support worker – whose light caseloads permit them to devote concentrated attention to the family, meeting them in the home three to four times a week. The emphasis is on 'parenting the parents' to help them in turn to nurture their children. Workers provide training in parental skills, mental health counselling, respite care, coaching in homemaking, budgeting assistance, help with job training and apartment-hunting, transportation, and support for substance abuse treatment. 'The work is focused on client strengths that can be mobilized to pursue the goals and plans that are the basis of the service provision' (p. 27).

Of 68 children whose cases were surveyed, 26 were reunified – a 'success rate' of 38% which the authors revise down to 28% after several children subsequently returned to care. Fein and Staff emphasise that *family reunification* work is much more difficult and demands a much more intensive use of resources than *family preservation* work. As they point out, 'sometimes family communication without cohabitation... is the best case resolution... Other times, the attempt to reunify is the last, best attempt at reasonable efforts to enable termination of parental rights to take place as a prelude to the permanency plan of adoption. Resisting the seduction of simple success measures to define complicated child welfare issues is vital, particularly in embracing new programs whose plans and ideals are attractive' (p. 39).

An earlier reunification programme which achieved a higher success rate, but possibly with a less difficult group of subjects, was the Alameda Project (Stein, Gambrill and Wiltse, 1978). This describes research carried out in California over twenty years ago and has already featured in other publications in this series (e.g. Macdonald and Roberts, 1995). However we have selected it for detailed description because it is the only example of a randomised controlled trial focused on continuity that we have been able to find. Despite obvious differences in legal and administrative conditions the findings of this study have much relevance to children who need to be looked after away from home in Britain today.

The primary objective of the project was to increase continuity of care for children placed away from home by court order. Intensive services were offered to birth parents to help them to participate effectively in decision-making and to improve their relationship with their children. Each child in the experimental group for whom no firm plan had yet been made was assigned jointly to a project worker and a county social worker. Children in the control group were allocated a county social worker only, in line with normal procedure. Four types of decisions were possible:

1.   Child restored to the birth parent(s).
2.   Child placed for adoption.
3.   Another adult designated as legal guardian.
4.   Child to remain in long-term foster placement

Continuity was defined as remaining in the same living situation for at least one year after the decision had been implemented. The first task of the project worker was to find out the parent's goal for the child's future. If a parent wanted the child returned to his or her care (as 95 per cent did), a case plan was drawn up in collaboration with the parent and county worker and a written contract agreed by all. Contracts were initially for 90 days with a possibility of renewal.

The research had two objectives: (i) to assess which decision resulted in greater stability for the child, and (ii) to test the effectiveness of case management using behavioural intervention methods to resolve identified problems.

The project lasted for two years with a follow up at the end of the third year. There were 227 children in the experimental group and 201 in the control group. Data were collected on children's characteristics, reasons for care, decision status for the child, contacts with birth parents, foster parents and other professionals. Methods used included analysis of records, monthly interviews, client-maintained records and direct observations by project workers in the natural environment. Characteristically for this time children's views are not recorded or mentioned.

Findings of the Alameda research

- By the end of year 2 of the project 79 per cent of the experimental group children compared with 40 per cent of the control group had left or were in the process of leaving foster care for one of the other three destinations. The third year follow-up showed that 98 per cent of these children had remained in the same home environment.

- Outcomes related to length of time in care and the type of work undertaken, not to the characteristics or history of the children.

- In the control group 60 per cent remained in long-term care, compared with 21 per cent in the experimental group.

- Although workers for both groups had approximately the same number of contacts with clients and other services, they were quite differently distributed. Experimental staff had far more contacts with birth parents. They were also much more likely to refer children for adoption.

- In cases where long-term care was the initial decision, placement changes occurred for nearly half the children. The authors conclude 'our data suggest that long-term (foster) care decisions are the least likely to result in continuity of care'.

- They suggest that the choice of long-term foster care often arises from social workers' reluctance to make decisions and lack of problem-solving skills rather than from objective assessment of the child's needs. In many cases the decision to opt for long-term care was used by social workers as a way of 'banking' cases as a form of caseload management, allowing them to give time to more immediate demands.

Implications for practice

In common with most later studies the authors found that the chances of a child either returning home or being adopted fell off steeply with time and were negligible after three years in care. The success of the Alameda project could be attributed to the intensive behavioural work with birth parents at an early stage in the placement. This would either result in progress or a well-evidenced decision that it could not be achieved. In the control group, once a decision was made that a child would require long-term care, services were directed almost entirely to foster carers rather than birth parents, thus creating a self-fulfilling prophecy. Work with parents by county workers consisted mostly of practical arrangements for contact visits rather than direct efforts to change the conditions which caused the child to require substitute care.

Many of the recommendations arising from the study are already common practice in this country to meet the requirements of the Children Act 1989. Others remain relevant and applicable, for example:

- making decisions based on parents' expressed wishes rather than social workers' views of their potential to be good parents.

- setting clear goals for what needs to change in the home and the relationship for the child to return, and setting them out in a written and signed contract.

- using highly structured behavioural methods in partnership with parent(s) to bring about the required change, and training child welfare social workers in the skills needed.

- close monitoring of cases to ensure that the care plan remains appropriate.

Perhaps the most important conclusion of this study is that long term foster care is inherently unstable and should only be used in specific cases as a positive choice, not as a default decision.

Reconnecting children and families

The reunification movement in the United States was criticised for making too great efforts to return children to families which continued to abuse or neglect them, and that has also been an anxiety in this country. Anthony Maluccio, who did so much to launch the movement, recognised the force of the child protection arguments and refined his original position by developing the concept of *connectedness*. Writing with various colleagues, he argues that child protection and family preservation are complementary goals. He redefined reunification as a planned process of *reconnecting* children in out-of-home care, not necessarily by returning them home to live, or even having frequent contact, but at some point along a spectrum which would help them to achieve and maintain an optimal level of reconnection in their particular circumstances. He argues for a flexible approach: 'not every parent can be a daily caregiver but some families, though not able to live together, can still maintain kinship bonds' so that children in foster care can remain members of their extended kinship system (Maluccio, Pine and Warsh, 1994; Maluccio, Fein and Davis, 1994). This perspective emphasises the importance of continuity, in this case of identity and family links, regardless of where the child may be living.

Kinship care

Another strategy is to make greater use of placements with relatives. In the USA, as we noted earlier, this is an increasingly important placement option. Mary Benedict and her colleagues studied family placement in Baltimore, USA (Benedict et al., 1996). They compared placements made with relatives with those made with strangers, looking for associations between the type of placement used and selected outcomes in adulthood. Interviews were conducted with 214 children formerly in care (40% kinship placed), who reported on parameters of their current functioning, including education and employment, physical and mental health, stresses and supports, and risk-taking behaviours. The authors found that children placed with relatives had fewer developmental, behaviour and mental health problems, better behaviour and attendance at school (although they did not achieve more) and greater stability – represented by fewer changes of placement. However, in adult life there were no differences between the two groups (86 placed with relatives, 128 placed with non-relatives). The authors were only able to speculate on the reasons. For instance, they suggest that relative carers may have poorer health, be less affluent or receive less support from social services. They refer to other studies showing the relative success of placement with relatives, with fewer placement changes although the length of stay is longer.

Maryjane Link's research in New York State also shows a high level of use of kinship placements leading to greater stability (Link, 1996). This was a longitudinal study of permanency planning for all 525 children placed in kinship foster care in Erie County, New York, in 1991. The author found that a high proportion of kinship placements led to permanence, in many cases through adoption. The largest number of placements were with maternal grandmothers, and made following proceedings for removal because of neglect. The article discusses a new approach, 'Kinship Options', being developed by the Erie County Department of Social Services to assure permanent family connections for children who come into contact with the child welfare system.

Concurrent planning

The Lutheran Social Services of Washington and Idaho have developed an approach called 'concurrent planning'. Lilian Katz reported on its apparent success in the journal *Adoption and Fostering* (Katz, 1996). She argues that:

● there are a number of severely pathological families who in reality offer little hope of successful reunification. (In an earlier publication (Katz and Robinson, 1991) she describes an assessment scheme with indicators which clearly distinguish such families from those who may, with intensive help and support, resume care of their children).

● most children who return home do so in first three months

● babies are at the highest risk of very long-term care

● the proportion of 'kinship' placements has doubled in the last ten years

- most children adopted from foster care are adopted by existing foster carers (80–90% according to her US figures).

Katz argues for *differential diagnosis*, leading in those cases where the chances of successful return are remote to immediate permanent placement, and where the prognosis is more hopeful but still poor, to *concurrent planning*. This means working for reunification while at the same time developing an alternative plan for placement with relatives or with foster carers who can adopt.

Katz claims that the agency's approach was initially treated with scepticism but that it has been successful in avoiding 'foster care drift'. Success depends on the existence of a large pool of prospective families willing to come forward and care for young children (0–8) with the hope of adoption but also the expectation of supporting a child's birth family during the foster care period and residually, after adoption. According to Katz her agency has been able to identify such a pool of families, although she acknowledges 'that their role is inevitably painful but necessary for the child's well-being.'

By 1987, six years after the start of the scheme, the Seattle children were moving from care to permanent homes within 13 months and by the mid 1990s this had fallen to nine months. It is estimated that 15 per cent of the children were able to return home, and 93 per cent of those adopted by permanency planning carers had only one placement (Katz and Robinson, 1991). The Manchester-based Goodman Project which has adopted this approach is described in the next chapter.

Inclusive practice

Sally Palmer analysed the placement experiences of 184 children looked after by Children's Aid Societies in Ontario, Canada (Palmer, 1996). Her research was based on theories of attachment and development regarding the importance of family relationships, and aimed to test such theories empirically by looking for links between 'inclusive practice' and placement stability. Inclusive practice was defined as treating parents as an important part of their children's lives – for instance by involving parents in the placement process and by helping children with their feelings about living apart from their families.

This careful study used intra-group comparison and regression analysis to compare the effect of a number of variables on stability. Palmer collected baseline information about the workers' training, experience and working practices. She collected data at the time of placement on the children's demographic characteristics, perceived difficulty of behaviour, main reason for being in care and parental attitude towards placement. She ascertained whether the child had a pre-placement visit, whether the parents were involved in preparation or in accompanying the child to the foster home, the child's level of family contact, and the foster carers' attitude to the child's parents. She then tracked the children for eighteen months following placement.

Of the 81 children who remained in care throughout the eighteen-month period 54% remained in their first placement, 27% had two homes, 14% three and 5% more than three. The variables most clearly associated with stability were the difficulty of the child's behaviour, the child's sex, parental involvement in preparation and the worker's training on the topic of separation (which paradoxically had an adverse effect). Contrary to the findings of other research, age was not associated with instability. (The ages of children studied ranged from 4 to 17 years.) Regression analysis showed that the strongest independent contributions appeared to be made by children's behaviour and parental preparation. Taken together, these two variables accounted for 20% of the total variation in placement stability; although the former greatly outweighed the latter.

In general Palmer found that 'inclusive practice' was the exception rather than the rule in the cases she studied and that 'in effect, workers appeared to have an inclusive approach in theory, but an exclusive approach in practice' (p. 599). Where they were able to put the theory into effect the placement was more likely to be stable. However, the association with the child's behaviour was much greater, and although Palmer suggests that this is something which workers cannot influence, it is possible that work to improve the child's behaviour, or to help the carers to manage it, may be an effective way to enhance placement stability.

Tony Tam and Mary Ho's findings from their study of 877 children placed in residential care in Hong Kong highlight the paramount importance of parental involvement in the child's prospect of returning home, and challenge decisions on discharge planning that do not take into account an overall view of the needs of the child concerned. The research, which used a structured questionnaire to social workers crosschecked with case records, repeats the frequent finding that parental contact is a powerful predictor of successful return home – but expands the notion of parental involvement to include not only contact but parental inclusion in pocket money, buying clothes, signing consent and so on. Continuity of care seems to make contact more meaningful, enhance the chances of reunification and lessen the negative effects of separation for the child.

Better support for carers

Patricia Chamberlain and her colleagues found a dramatic improvement in foster care retention rates associated with increased payments and additional support. In this experiment one group of foster carers received enhanced support and training including additional payments, another received additional payments only, and a control group were assessed in the normal way. Over two years the dropout rate from foster care was 9.6% for the enhanced support and training group, 14.3% for the group receiving increased payments only, and 25.9% for the control group (Chamberlain et al., 1993).

Key points from Chapter 6

- The links between stability and continuity are complex and subtle. Frequently the two go together; sometimes they do not.

- Research into children's views indicates that they often have little choice over changes of placement. The impact of disruption to their social networks can be traumatic.

- We review a number of initiatives that have been taken in an effort to improve stability for children who are looked after:
  - Family and adolescent support services
  - Reunification programmes
  - 'Kinship care'
  - 'Concurrent planning'
  - 'Inclusive practice'
  - Better support for carers.

CHAPTER 7 : PROMISING IDEAS

In this chapter we look more closely at several pieces of innovative practice in which people have attempted to provide a more secure future for children and young people. Questions that arise in relation to these schemes are:

> What is the evidence that they are effective?
> What essential features enable them to provide greater stability (if they do)?
> Do they have any lessons for mainstream services?
> Are they replicable?

We start with Pro-Teen, a specialist fostering scheme which is one of the longest established in the UK and the only one as far as we know to have been formally evaluated.

Pro-Teen

Pro-Teen developed from the Kent Family Placement Project set up in 1975 to pioneer the then adventurous idea of placing difficult adolescents, including offenders, in foster families instead of residential settings. It became an independent agency in 1988 when the families involved felt that the bureaucracy associated with local government management was getting in the way of the service they wanted to provide for young people. To provide continuity is one of the main aims of the agency, which has served as a model for a number of similar specialist services, both in the United Kingdom and in other countries. We describe Pro-Teen at the time of writing. An account of its history and development can be found in a book edited by Nancy Hazel and Andrew Fenyo, *Free to be Myself: the development of teenage fostering* (Hazel and Fenyo, 1993).

Pro-Teen is a self-governing association of 20 foster families. It has two professional workers and administrative support. Otherwise it is run entirely by the foster families themselves, buying in additional professional services as needed. The fees, though not high by private agency standards, are set to cover the standard payment to families (per child placed), the support workers' salaries, and all other expenses needed to provide a high quality service tailored to each young person's individual needs.

The agency is managed by a Board of Trustees/Directors consisting of four independent members with business, educational and charity experience plus three Pro-Teen foster carers elected by the families and a representative from each of the other two standing committees of the organisation. The Professional Committee is made up of four elected Pro-Teen carers and four members from a social work background, one of whom is on the support staff. The third committee, composed of five elected foster carers promotes and organises after care. Support groups and workshops meet two or three times a month and there is also a monthly group meeting for own children of foster carers called 'Natural Children United' run by someone who was herself brought up as the birth child of a foster family.

The group of families which constitute Pro-Teen is very stable, some having been with the project since the beginning. New families have to understand and buy into the philosophy of the project and visit all the other families, who feed back their views and reactions to the Professional Committee, which makes the final decision about who should be accepted. It is considered very important that Pro-Teen families spend time together and think about how far they share ideas about the care and management of young people. They can then feel comfortable about passing on the care of a child if it should become necessary. That possibility is envisaged from the start so that a family who feel they cannot continue to provide a home for a particular young person need not feel a failure. Families are approved for a fixed number of children – two if one foster carer does not work outside the home, three if two foster carers are available full-time.

The agency has a positive approach to the problem of non-school attenders and unemployed school-leavers which so often leads to breakdown of conventional foster placements. The Pro-Teen families are resourceful in getting and maintaining previously hard to educate and unemployable young people into school and work, but if this is not achieved within a short time the Educational/Vocational Activities organiser develops an individual programme for the young person. Tutors and activity-providers work with the teenager on a one-to-one basis in conjunction with the foster carers to fill educational gaps and provide training in social and life skills. The very flexible programme is aimed at integration back into mainstream schooling or work attendance.

Either the child or the family must give 28 days notice of a wish to end the placement. This provides a cooling-off period during which difficulties can be tackled and alternative arrangements considered. If the problems in the placement cannot be immediately resolved a respite placement may be arranged with another family. Otherwise continuity can be achieved by a transfer within the Pro-Teen group to a family which is likely to be already well-known to the young person. This transfer system is one of the most important features of the service and depends on a group of limited size working closely together to a common purpose. This, according to the support worker, overcomes the problem of the family who had to pass on the child feeling a failure and the receiving family, if they succeed, feeling omnipotent. 'It is achieving the goal that counts, not expecting the person who kicked off to score.'

Another element of stability is provided by the commitment to indefinite after-care, which consists of much more than telephone calls and moral support. Foster carers are able to make decisions within broad guidelines about what is needed to help their young person over a difficult time. For example, carers will travel long distances to help a former resident going through a crisis, reclaiming their expenses from the After-Care Committee without needing to ask for advance authorisation. They may provide temporary accommodation for 'ex-placements', lend money for deposits or rent in advance, help with wedding expenses, take former foster children and their children on holiday – in other words demonstrate the kind of continuing support and concern most families offer their adult children. It is quite common for teenagers who have lived independently for a while to return to their former carers for 'relaunching'. The general view among Pro-Teen carers is that local authority social workers greatly over-estimate the ability of young people to cope alone at an early age.

Evaluation

How far does the Pro-Teen service succeed in creating greater stability than these young people might otherwise have experienced? Hazel (1993) comments that it is difficult to assess success and failure since 'measures such as "breakdown" or "improved in placement" are both incomplete and short-term' (p.12). A much longer-term follow up would be needed to establish the superiority of the Pro-Teen model over other forms of care. However, the service is probably unique in having been formally evaluated four times, each time showing significantly better outcomes than other forms of placement, with young people who, by definition, are especially difficult to help. Studies by Yelloly (1979) and Hazel (1981) came up with closely similar findings, with 60 per cent of placements completed as planned compared with less than half for traditional fostering, and 70 per cent of the young people considered to have improved during placement. The fourth study, by the Personal Social Services Research Unit at the University of Kent (Fenyo, Knapp and Baines, 1989) used more sophisticated research methodology but found a very similar proportion of breakdowns – 38 per cent. None of these evaluations attempted to assess the effect on these vulnerable young people's subsequent experience of having a reliable, lasting relationship with a caring adult, something that Pro-Teen, unlike local authority fostering, aims to provide.

No more recent evaluation has been carried out, but an analysis of placement statistics supplied by Pro-Teen covering the period April 1989 to March 1998 suggests that the relative success of the service in creating stability for looked after young people has been maintained. Over these nine years 265 placements were provided, of which only 57 ended in an unplanned way, and in 21 of those cases the young people concerned returned to their own families. There were 71 transfers within Pro-Teen (in one case the same girl transferring six times), which in conventional fostering would probably have been counted and experienced as breakdowns.

Many of the placements were only planned to be short-term, but 39 per cent of the young people who left their placements during these years had lived at least one year in the same place and many of them for more than three years. This represents much greater stability than is usually reported for teenagers, especially those in residential care (see, for example, Triseliotis, Borland et al., 1995). The foster families also appeared to be very stable, no more than one or two retiring in any year, though 17 families joined over the nine year period.

The circumstances of the young people looked after by Pro-Teen foster families are mostly extremely complex and they make great demands on the skill and tolerance of their carers. The figures on termination of placements are hard to interpret since much depends on the policy of the placing local authority and how much importance is given to stability and continuity. For instance, if young people's needs appear to have diminished some authorities may decide to place them with less costly local authority carers without regard to the disruptive effect of a move. A follow up study of Pro-Teen leavers comparing them with conventionally fostered young people from the same authorities would be extremely valuable.

The Children's Family Trust

The Children's Family Trust (CFT) is a long-established independent charitable organisation which offers a unique model of substitute care for children who are not able to live with their families. It was set up with the explicit purpose of providing long-term stability and security for separated children.

Becoming a CFT family is a lifetime commitment. CFT Parents undertake to look after up to ten children including their own from the time the child joins their family to adulthood and beyond. There is no cut-off point. The children leave home when they feel ready but continue to look for help and advice to their Parents. Their sibling network, made up of birth and CFT brothers and sisters, also continues to be available both for emotional support and practical help. The sense of group identity which is fostered by the CFT model is itself a source of support, and relationships between Parents and grown-up children become increasingly reciprocal as they get older. The Trust provides housing of an appropriate size for the family and meets major capital costs; running costs are met by the Parents out of the income they receive via the Trust for caring for the children. Sometimes one of the couple works outside the home, at least part-time.

The care provided by the Trust does not fit easily into any familiar category. It is quite unlike the standard model of residential care. There are no 'staff', no rotas: CFT Parents provide full-time care, 24 hours a day, arranging relief for themselves just like ordinary parents, using babysitters, friends and grandparents and paying for domestic help as needed. The aim is for the CFT family to be as much like any other family as possible. The house carries no indication that it has any special function. The telephone number is listed in the directory under the Parents' name, not under 'Children's Family Trust'.

The service has some features in common with professional or specialist fostering. Most of the children placed with CFT families have suffered extremely traumatic experiences, having been severely abused, neglected or abandoned, and the fees charged to local authorities reflect the difficulty of looking after them. However, in contrast to many specialist fostering schemes, these are not time-limited placements for one or two years. Agencies placing children through CFT do so on the understanding that the children will not be moved except at their own request and are expected to remain in their family until they reach adulthood.

The CFT model also has some of the characteristics of exclusive or quasi-adoptive fostering – deeply unfashionable at present. For example, children may use their CFT family name at school, and usually prefer to do so. They may call the Parents and refer to them as mum and dad, and their foster siblings as brothers and sisters. On the other hand the children are not cut off from their birth families, and unless there are strong reasons against it they are encouraged to stay in communication with family members who are important to them. At least two-thirds of children have some contact with relatives, usually parents. When they ask questions about their past they are answered openly and honestly, even if the truth is painful. If they become interested in knowing more about their birth family or culture they are given all the help they need. CFT Parents looking after a black child with no relative contact found him an independent visitor from the same ethnic background.

The family builds up gradually to the maximum number, often including several sibling pairs. Over a third of the children come together with a brother or sister, especially in the early stages, but later vacancies tend to come singly. Adding a new member to the family is a very important decision in which everyone is involved. Care is taken that the child really wants to come and feels that he or she can be comfortable living in the family home.

Outcomes

Unfortunately no independent evaluation of the Children's Family Trust has yet been carried out, despite the fact that it has been in existence for over half a century and has brought up at least 250 children, most of whom remain in touch with their CFT Parents, brothers and sisters. There are two published accounts of the model which provide a very clear description of how the system differs from conventional foster or residential care and offer some evidence of its success in creating stability (Cairns, 1984, Cairns and Cairns, 1989).

Children are placed with CFT because the plan for them is permanent substitute care: their parents are judged unlikely ever to be able to look after them to an acceptable standard. By this time they are usually aged at least four and sometimes much older, have experienced many previous placements – 18 separate admissions to care in the case of one brother and sister – and are considered not only unsuitable for adoption but also unsuitable for mainstream fostering because of their highly disturbed behaviour. In other words they fall into the group of children at highest risk of further placement breakdown. However, analysis of outcomes for the first 201 CFT children showed a success rate of 96%. 16 children were reunited with birth parents (several after more than five years) and only eight placements broke down. In every case these were older children deciding to leave the CFT family, not as a result of rejection by CFT Parents.

An interesting point raised by Brian Cairns (1984) is that CFT Parents have three 'own' children on average, and families may well include 'placed' children close in age and of the same sex. In Roy Parker's classic study of 1966 this was a high risk factor for placement breakdown, and his findings have been repeatedly confirmed. However, it does not seem to apply in CFT families. Cairns argues that there are specific advantages in the large size of the CFT family in which relationships between the children may be as important as those between the child and either Parent and the impact of individual competition is diluted. Nevertheless it remains a potential problem, and in creating their own family Brian and Kate Cairns tried to avoid having children of the same sex in the same school year (Cairns and Cairns, 1989).

An examination of outcomes for 15 children who have grown up in one CFT family underlines the point that stability does not just lie in continuity of placement but also in achieving a sustainable adult life-style. In contrast to most careleavers (Broad, 1998), all the children attended school at least until 16 and obtained some GCSEs or equivalent and 11 continued into further or higher education. This was achieved by close liaison with local schools and by giving education in its broadest sense high priority within the home. All the family members are in employment at the time of writing, except for one who has a college place for 1999. They have a wide variety of occupations: maintenance engineer, sales director, canteen supervisor, dairyman, airline administrator, publisher, professional footballer. For many of them (the eldest now 33) life has not run smoothly, but the continuing emotional security provided by the CFT family seems to have enabled them to overcome difficulties, make relationships, and find a place for themselves in mainstream society.

How can we account for the success of the CFT in creating stability? It cannot be attributed to earlier placement since most children are between 8 and 14 when they join their families, nor to their being easier to look after – even after many years the behaviour of some is unpredictable and occasionally violent. The effects of early trauma seem often to be re-experienced in adolescence, and a tantrum which would be merely tiresome in a three-year-old can be dangerous and frightening at thirteen; it is no accident that this is the stage when so many conventional foster placements break down.

The Children's Family Trust is a Christian organisation, and many of the Parents are inspired by religious conviction, though this varies greatly in outward expression from family to family. They are helped through difficult times by regular monthly visits from a member of the Trust Council, and they also receive support from the CFT professional worker and, to a greater or lesser extent, from local authority social workers. For many families the most valuable support has come from other CFT Parents, despite their geographical spread.

CFT Parents typically have a higher level of education than is usual among foster parents and some have professional qualifications. One CFT couple undertook social work training in successive years, each supporting the other by assuming the main responsibility for caring while their partner was studying. Parents are very carefully selected, and most enquirers eliminate themselves once they understand what they would be undertaking. When the decision is made to start a new family it may take the Trust a year or more to find the right couple.

There are many other features of the Children's Family Trust which contribute to its success in creating a stable environment for separated children. These include the model of family life provided by the Parents, the fact that they live their lives and pursue their own interests in the common living space, not in some separate place in their 'free' time. Another important element is the involvement of family members in a wide variety of activities in the local community as opposed to the tokenism of most 'community' homes.

The question arises, should not these children for whom reunification is generally not an option, have been placed for adoption? It may well be that some of them should have been, especially if this could have happened at a much earlier age. However Cairns (1984) argues that CFT may offer a better chance of placement stability and other forms of continuity to some children who have already been severely damaged by abuse, neglect and repeated rejection.

The reasons that he advances for this conclusion are: the unavailability of adequate post-adoption social work support, the fact that adoptive parents usually have less experience than CFT Parents of dealing with very disturbed children, and that even if adoption allowances are paid they are unlikely to approach the level of professional fostering fees. Moreover, adoptive families are normally small and generate a degree of emotional intensity which many of these children are unable to tolerate.

Could the CFT approach be expanded or replicated to serve more children? This might be a possibility, provided it was not smothered by bureaucracy or additional layers of administration. There have always been many differences between one CFT family and another. The success seems to lie in the overall model and vision and the lifelong commitment of Parents rather than in details of practical application or the efficiency of the organisation. Any change which undermined this philosophy would risk reducing the model to no more than a collection of small children's homes or a network of specialist foster carers.

The Goodman Project

This is a scheme set up by the Manchester Adoption Society (MAS) in conjunction with Bury and Salford Social Services Departments to try to reduce the number of moves experienced by children before they are eventually adopted. An study of 27 cases referred to MAS over a six-month period during 1996/7 discovered that 17 of the children had moved no less than four times before adoption. This is in line with Gilles Ivaldi's finding that it is common for children adopted from care to experience multiple changes of placement; 11 per cent of those adopted in 1997 had five or more changes and a further 25 per cent had at least three (Ivaldi, 1998).

The project, funded by the Pilgrim Trust, the Hayward Foundation and the Department of Health is based on the system known as 'concurrent planning' developed in Seattle, USA, where it has been in operation since 1981 (see chapter 6). Prospective adopters work initially as foster carers alongside social workers to reunite foster children with their birth families. If the attempt fails they undertake to adopt the foster child. The aim is to create stability and security for the child, either with their own family or with a new permanent family with which they are already familiar. No further moves would be necessary before adoption.

The British scheme is still in its early stages but, as described in the last chapter, there is good evidence from America that suitable families willing to live with uncertainty can be found and that concurrent permanency planning can reduce the number of moves for children before adoption, and in that way increase the chances that the adoption will be successful. The project is being independently evaluated by the Thomas Coram Research Unit.

'Next Steps'

'Next Steps' is a Newcastle-based initiative which attempts to create some stability for a small number of very troubled young people with long term needs who have exhausted most available placement options. It is designed to help the minority of children aged 13–16 who otherwise risk suffering from repeated placement breakdowns and associated crisis moves. These are children are beyond the scope of Family and Adolescent Support Services (described in Chapter 6) either because they have suffered from serious abuse within their families or because of their own extreme behaviour.

Criteria for referral to the Next Steps team include such factors as self-harm or suicidal behaviour, substance or alcohol misuse, being extremely aggressive, offending, referral for secure accommodation, non-school-attendance, abuse issues, multiple agency involvement, low self-esteem and self-defeating behaviour. Normally many of these factors would coincide and interact. The four-person Next Steps team works with a strictly limited number of young people in collaboration with the allocated local authority social worker.

Placement stability and reduction in crisis placement requests is a prime objective of the project, achieved by a fast response service which provides help when and where it is needed. The Next Steps workers aim to provide support and advocacy in relation to all the various agencies engaged with the participants. They use a range of approaches which include groupwork both with the young people and their families, cognitive-behavioural and anger control methods, and individualised support and advice, making use of services and consultancy from relevant professionals in other agencies.

The basic principles of the service are:

- All intervention should be based on clear planning and on aims and objectives mutually agreed with social workers, parents, young people and any other relevant agencies or placements.

- Intervention is continuous over 12–18 months, following the young person wherever they are placed. Next Steps recognises that with this group of teenagers crises are to be expected but, in contrast to common practice, are not to be resolved by rejection of the young person, setting up the next placement to fail yet again.

- Next Steps promotes an understanding that it is normal to experience difficulty in parenting or caring for troubled young people.

- The service works in partnership with young people on the basis of openness and honesty in decision making processes.

Next Steps is funded on an annual basis and plans to adopt a continuous monitoring and evaluation approach to test whether it is meeting its stated objectives. However no outcome data are yet available.

Barnardo's Family Placement Services, Edinburgh

This service was set up in 1992, bringing together two previous projects. One had provided time-limited, task-centred foster care aiming for the child to return to birth parents or as a bridge to long-term placement, and the other arranged permanent family placements for older and disabled children The aim in developing an integrated service was to offer maximum possible continuity and stability for children by providing a full continuum of services from respite care to adoption without the need to transfer children from one placement to another for administrative reasons.

The project was based on research findings showing the large number of moves that children had experienced before placement with Barnardo's (see Hughes, 1996) and the evidence that disruption was less likely when a permanent placement was made with foster carers who had previously cared for the child. Like the Goodman Project described above, it also makes use of the concurrent planning approach developed by Linda Katz (Katz and Robinson, 1991).

Family Placement Services set specific targets for increasing the continuity of care experienced by children placed with the project and has carefully monitored outcomes. The most recent figures show that they have surpassed their targets, so that 97% of children placed by the service have had no more than one main move and 81.5% have had only one respite carer. This suggests that the project is achieving far greater stability for children than local authority child care services are able to do at present.

It also provides important evidence that foster carers can be found who are willing to work on a concurrent planning model. Although this is particularly demanding for the carers it appears that it delivers better outcomes and greater continuity for children. In the case described below the child was returned to his birth mother, but had things turned out differently he would have been permanently fostered or adopted by the foster carers, and that may still be the long-term outcome. This is how it looks from the carers' perspective:

We have been fostering for Barnardo's for nearly ten years. We have had some really difficult placements but the task we have embarked on just now is probably the most difficult.

> We went through the usual – getting papers, meeting the child's social worker. Then things changed with the child's plan. Instead of a permanent placement we were asked if we could rehabilitate this child with his mum, but if it fell through could we keep him long-term?

> It was a shock and in some respects asking too much of us. We were aware that we must somehow get close enough to let him know we are here in case it doesn't work out with mum, but not so close in case we influence him to stay here with us. What particularly helps is our realisation of the strength and importance of birth parents. Our own family is reconstituted and we are aware that nothing compensates for the loss of a parent however much we give to a child. The belief that children should be with their birth parents helped us decide to give this our best shot.

> We are sure he finds it difficult listening to mixed messages, comparing two families etc. His mum lacks skills in containing

and looking after him appropriately, which leads to worry about how the family will manage. It's complex and difficult to keep him on track, yet we are hoping for the best, and we will also be prepared if necessary to support his birth family long-term on a shared care basis.

Key points from chapter 7

Because these projects are innovative and experimental, there is in general little hard evidence of how effective they are in comparison with other kinds of service provision. Nonetheless, in an area of practice where there is so much uncertainty about what works, it is worth sharing information about projects that are at least believed to be effective by those involved in them, and that are based on sound principles and clear thinking. Returning to the questions with which we started this chapter, can we see any common features in the schemes described above?

● All make stability and continuity an explicit goal.

● One thing that all the projects have in common is that they are outside the structure of mainstream social services. They are not constrained by conventional boundaries and aim to access any appropriate services on behalf of the young people in their care.

● All allow first-hand carers or workers in regular contact with young people considerable autonomy to use resources in the way that seems most important to them. This in turn allows them to act quickly and decisively to meet needs or defuse crises.

● They are committed to involving young people in decisions about their lives, giving them a sense of responsibility for themselves and enhancing their self-esteem.

● Most aim to provide continuing support into young adulthood, so that leaving care is not an abrupt event but a gradual process in which independence can be achieved at the individual's own pace and with the understanding that even competent, well-functioning young people need a refuge from time to time. It is one of the weaknesses of local authority care that this kind of after-care support is so seldom available.

CHAPTER 8 : RESEARCH, PRACTICE AND POLICY

The original purpose of this short book was to draw together the findings of research in order to provide clear, objective and well-founded indicators of what kind of practice is most likely to promote and maintain stability for looked after children. Our success in doing this has been limited for a number of reasons. First, we have seen that there has been little research which directly addresses questions of stability, and some of the most important studies date from before the implementation of the Children Act 1989. Second (and the preceding factor may be connected with this), researching stability is a difficult and complex undertaking if the aim is to produce quantifiable information. The subject does not lend itself to experimental methods; the variables involved can be difficult to disentangle; and defining stability is not a simple matter. Therefore many of the findings reported here are ambiguous or drawn from qualitative studies with small samples which may not be representative. There is no research which puts stability for looked after children at the centre, and very little which provides clear information on moves *within* care, the causes of instability or what can be done to reduce it. Almost all the research suffers from a fundamental weakness when we look for answers on what creates stability: in discussing breakdown rates it confounds age at placement and age of placement breakdown, so when we are told that 50 per cent of adolescent foster placements fail we do not know if these are young people in care since the age of three or teenagers in conflict with their families whose first placement was at 13. Staff and Fein (1995) found a similar problem with the American literature, noting how few studies specifically address the subject of children's placement stability while in care. They remark, however, that despite methodological incompatibilities and flawed data, these few studies 'command our attention; they define the enormity of the phenomenon of placement change'.

Third, even where evidence is available it can be difficult to interpret and to use in practice. To take one example, the connection between older age of a child at placement and the likelihood of breakdown is very well established – but what exactly are its implications for practice? One cannot make children younger. Should we be removing them earlier from their families, which cuts across other objectives and indeed goes against the fundamental philosophy behind the Children Act? Should we be resisting the removal of older children from their families more strongly? What does it mean for practice with an individual child to know that her theoretical risk of placement breakdown is higher than it would have been had she been three years younger, when her circumstances mean that she still needs a placement to be made? We cannot manipulate child care policies to ensure that we only place those children who are most likely to succeed, because the service for looking after children is necessarily a reactive one for much of the time.

A related example is of a research finding that has been acted on. This is the repeated finding that children placed with carers who have a child of the same age or younger are at higher risk of rejection. This finding has been well known in practice for a number of years and undoubtedly has had an effect on placement decisions. How do these decisions then feed back into subsequent research? Are children only being placed in such situations where there are other factors which increase the chances of success – for instance, the level of experience of the foster carers? Or are they only being placed where there is no alternative or when practitioners do not know of the research findings? The way in which practitioners are or are not taking into account previous research may be important in understanding the meaning of subsequent findings.

Nevertheless we have found some useful indicators for practice and for management. Some of them may seem obvious, while others are more surprising. We have also found – or are able to deduce – some directions in which policy may need to change if looked after children are to be given the best chance of stability. In this chapter we summarise some of these lessons for practice, for management and for policy. First we need to review what we have learned about what works to promote and maintain stability and what works against it.

Lessons for practice

When we looked at the factors that have been found to be associated with stability and instability, we found some which have featured repeatedly in research while others only appear in one or two studies. We summarise the main ones below: first the negative factors, then the positive ones. It should be borne in mind of course that association does not necessarily imply causation. The care population includes an enormous variety of children, from babies placed for adoption to 17 year-olds escaping from an oppressive family, and a range of complex family situations which affect social work plans and children's lives in unpredictable ways. Social workers need to be aware of research findings, but they can never replace professional judgement in individual cases.

Some of the main factors contributing to instability

Strongly supported by research findings

- placement at older age

- child's behaviour seen as problematic by carers

- placement in residential unit with frequent emergency admissions

- school problems, especially if leading to exclusion

- child separated from siblings

- foster parents' children very young or close in age to foster child

- lack of social work support

- exclusion of birth parents from placement

- child has history of abuse or neglect

- early stage of placement

- poor coordination of services

Less strongly supported

- conflicting expectations between carers and social workers

- child under care order

- transracial foster placements

- child of mixed parentage

Main factors contributing to stability

Strongly supported

- adoption, especially if under 4 years

- remaining with own family despite difficulties

- returning home within six months

- placement with relatives

- school success

- intensive social work support during early stages of placement

- absence of behaviour problems

- maintaining child's social networks

- placement with siblings

- previous acquaintance with foster parents

- parental involvement in child's life

- older, more experienced foster carers

- higher rates of payment for fostering

Less strongly supported (e.g. single studies)

- child's participation in decision-making

- short period in residential care before foster placement

- other foster children in family

- early warning system and negotiation before acceptance of breakdown

- parental involvement in preparation for placement

- change in designation of an existing short-term placement

- devolution of authority to long-term foster parents

- specialised family placement section in social services

Implications for practice

These findings suggest that, whether we are looking for a permanent placement for a child or working with children whose stay in the care system is intended to be temporary, there are some common elements of good practice:

- Staying at home offers the best chance of stability: family preservation has a higher success rate than reunification (but this has to be balanced against the risk of harm to the child).

- Placement with relatives is preferable to placement with strangers if a suitable person is available and willing, and every effort should be made to find such a person and overcome any obstacles.

- For school age children equal attention should be given to the school placement and the care placement. The school should be informed of any change of placement (including from home to accommodation) and its implications for the child discussed. *Continuity* of school placement and education should receive very high priority.

- For children with more difficulties we should look for carers with previous experience

- Long-term placements with carers who have young children close in age to the child to be placed are to be avoided. If there are strong reasons for such a placement the implications need to be fully discussed with the foster parents

- The child's existing social networks should be maintained as far as possible in the new placement

- Siblings should stay together unless there are strong reasons to the contrary.

- We should ensure that there is good preparation for the placement, and that parents are positively involved as much as possible both in the preparation and in the placement

- We should build in a solid pattern of social work support for carers, for parents and for the child, right from the start of the placement

- Where children have particular difficulties extra support should be planned from the start, rather than waiting for things to go wrong

As we have seen, there is more than one kind of stability for looked after children, and the answer to the question 'how do we achieve stability?' may be different in each case. There is *long term stability* in the sense of a permanent home with the same family or group of people, as part of the same community and culture, and with long term continuity of relationships and identity. For a significant number of children who are looked after, the question how best to achieve this long term stability – with the child's birth family or with a new one, by fostering or by adoption, by making the best of the child's present situation or by searching for an better one – is the key decision that has to be made on the basis of careful assessment. But *short or medium term stability or continuity* in the sense of avoiding unnecessary disruption to a child's life may be an important issue both for children who are going to need new permanent arrangements and for the many children whose stay in the care system is predictably brief. How many changes of placement, of school, of doctor; how many separations from friends and family; how many uncertainties and unwelcome surprises a child has to contend with, may make a huge difference to the quality of his or her life while in the system and after leaving it.

With both long and short term stability some of the factors which make for success may be beyond the control of social workers or anyone else involved in the day-to-day care of looked after children. We look first at those factors that are to some degree within our control. In relation to both long and short term stability we suggest that the following are of critical importance.

A clear and focused planning process

From the point of admission the question of how to establish and maintain long-term stability for the child should be at the forefront of everyone's minds. This requires a realistic and systematic assessment of the likely capacity of the family to provide a permanent home for the child. In order to avoid keeping the child in limbo for an indefinite period it is essential to make contingency or concurrent plans which can be acted on rapidly as soon as the evidence is available to make a decision.

Considering adoption

The evidence is overwhelmingly strong that adoption offers the best hope of long-term stability, a family for life, for *any* child whose birth family is unlikely to be able to provide adequate care within a defined space of time. Adoption has a much better record of providing stability than open-ended foster care, and many previous difficulties have been overcome with the move to open adoption and payment of allowances. Where the plan for a child is long-term care, social workers should ask themselves if there is any good reason why the child should *not* be placed for adoption.

The latest government circular *Adoption – Achieving the Right Balance* (DoH, 1998a) takes a stronger position on this than any previous official guidance.

> Adoption is not an option of last resort; to regard it as such is a failure to understand the nature of adoption and its advantages for a child unable to live with his own family. ...Adoption provides children with a unique opportunity for a fresh start as permanent members of new families, enjoying a sense of security and well-being so far denied them in their young lives (p.2).

The circular urges local authorities to take a realistic and time-limited approach to rehabilitation, not attempting to exhaust all other possibilities. It also makes it clear that considerations such as ethnic origin and religion or the wishes of the birth family should take second place to the need of the child for a permanent family at the earliest point possible. Strategic plans for children's services should 'place adoption firmly at the centre of options available for the long-term care of children' and there should be a less restrictive attitude to the acceptance of would-be adoptive parents. The research we have reviewed in this book gives strong support to the government's policy on adoption as set out in the Circular.

Clear plans for contact between children, parents and other relatives

Contact aimed at eventual return must be clearly distinguished from contact designed to ensure continuity of relationship or what Anthony Maluccio has called 'connectedness'. The *quality* of contact is also crucial – too often the focus is on practical arrangements, when ensuring that the contact is enjoyable and interesting for both adults and children is the most important task. In many cases, where the child is adopted or in a settled long-term foster placement, it may be more appropriate for contact to take the form of information exchange rather than face-to-face encounters.

Individualised choice of placement

Careful selection of a placement to suit a particular child or children may be a counsel of perfection but is strongly associated with stability. When children have to be placed with whoever is available then there is a good likelihood that things will go wrong. When children and foster parents feel they have chosen each other they are more likely to be committed to sticking with the placement through difficult times. There are legal and rights-based reasons for involving children as fully as possible in decision-making about placement, but it is also most likely to result in a successful placement. We are very far from achieving this at present (Fletcher, 1993, Shaw, 1998).

Geographical location is another important factor. We have emphasized the importance of continuity in schooling, but when because of a placement change this involves a long daily journey keeping a child at the same school can be self-defeating. Children operate within a very small area and it is almost impossible to preserve their social networks when they are moved any distance.

Keeping siblings together

When two or more siblings are separated from their principal attachment figure the distress of each may be diminished by interaction with the other (Heinicke and Westheimer, 1965), The protective, caregiving role played by the older sibling may actually help her to feel more secure herself. Even a child of preschool age may serve as an attachment figure to a younger sibling. This may explain why placements with siblings are more stable than when brothers and sisters are separated. However, there are some contrary research findings which stress the importance of listening to children. Some siblings may not be helpful to each other, as in the case of a girl who was placed despite her protests with her older half brother who had previously abused her physically and subjected her to racist taunts.

Social work support for foster carers and birth parents

If social workers do not have the time or the skills to provide support to the placement from the beginning, problems are likely to build up before there is a chance for good relationships to develop. This probably accounts for the tendency of placements to break down more often in their early stages. There is much evidence that once a placement is made social work attention is rapidly switched in another direction. However, agencies which are more successful in creating stability provide intensive social work report right at the start of the placement. Equally, intensive work is required with the birth family. Families may want to change in a way that will enable them to keep their children but not know how to do so without help. Only by active work with the family is it impossible to make an informed assessment of whether to plan for return home or for long-term care. Either way, the placement is more likely to be successful if the birth parents are fully involved.

Preventing disruption

Jane Aldgate and David Hawley made some helpful suggestions for improving practice and preventing placement breakdown as a result of their retrospective study of 20 failed placements (Aldgate and Hawley, 1986):

1. Before placement, make a meticulous, well documented assessment of the child. Include material from direct observation of his or her behaviour. Be honest with yourself and foster parents about the child's difficulties.

2. Try to place the child in a family who can build on the past. Compensation for poor experiences is important but continuity with positives should take priority.

3. Help foster families assess for themselves what they have to offer. Accept this at face value and do not try to bend it to fit the child's needs, however desperate you may be.

4.	Establish an open relationship with foster parents by sharing information with them, explaining behaviour difficulties in context, with examples. Throughout the placement continue this relationship by involving foster parents in reviews and important decisions affecting their foster child's life.

5.	Prepare children for their placement through life story books and other techniques so that they are ready for the move. Involve former foster carers and birth parents in this process. Take account of foster parents' instincts to establish optimal timing for the beginning of the placement.

6.	Make sure the goals of the placement are clear and communicated verbally and in writing to everyone concerned. Provide evidence of why decisions have been made in writing and establish clear channels of communication for foster parents, children and their birth parents.

7.	Define the purpose and frequency of access for birth parents and ensure that clear agreements are made and upheld between all parties.

8.	Visit the placement frequently in the early stages, even if all seems well.

9.	Be honest, admit to foster parents if you do not know the answer to their problems but try to link them to others who can help.

10.	Do not run away from signs of trouble: anticipate crises and have a strategy for dealing with them.

Promoting continuity

As we have tried to show throughout this report, discontinuity is one of the most damaging effects of placement change, and needs to be tackled as an issue in itself. The Department of Health's Looking After Children materials, discussed in Chapter 6, are an essential tool for improving continuity of care, providing a guide to the many different areas of a child's life which may be disrupted by a placement move. The high risk of placement disruption, which we cannot ignore, makes it all the more essential that both the administrative forms and Assessment and Action Records are fully completed and discussed in detail with the new carer when a move is unavoidable. A very frequent complaint of both foster parents and residential workers is that children are placed without the carers being given any information about them.

Although the LAC materials have been adopted by almost all UK local authorities, research on the impact of the implementation on practice is not yet complete. Their effectiveness as a practice tool to provide better quality of care and greater continuity for looked after children will depend both on the way they are used by social workers and on the extent to which they are supported in this by managers.

Lessons for management

The key factors

From our review of the research and our discussions with practitioners three things stood out as necessary if there is to be a real improvement in stability and continuity of care for looked after children. The first sounds obvious but is not part of current social services management practice. That is to make stability the default option. It should be assumed that once a placement decision has been made the child or young person will stay in that place for as long as planned, unless there are the strongest possible reasons why they should move. Lord Laming, speaking at the House of Commons shortly before his retirement as Chief Social Services Inspector, said categorically that no child should be moved except in the interests of her own welfare, and certainly not for financial or administrative reasons. If all social services departments were to adopt this as policy the current instability of placement would be dramatically reduced (see also the discussion of Norwegian policy below).

However, stability also depends on there being *choice of placement*. So often children have to be placed wherever is available at the time, and choice appears to be a luxury. However well social workers are trained in assessing children's needs, in making sound collaboratively-based plans, in matching children to carers, in identifying those children for whom residential care is a positive choice, all this is wasted if placement resources are so scarce that these processes are irrelevant. Many of the placements that break down are those made in an emergency or for want of anything better, in many cases placements which are acknowledged from the beginning to be inappropriate or unlikely to last.

In both foster care and residential care clearer distinctions need to be made between placements designed to provide temporary refuge and those that aim to provide a long-term home for a child. If residential care is to be a serious possibility we need to revive the notion of group living as a positive option for some children, but it can only be that if it provides a home for as long as they need it, one which will not be unpredictably invaded by outsiders in crisis or subject to constant turnover of residents and staff. The implications of this for management are fairly clear: they need completely to rethink their current model of residential care and the quality of staffing required both for short-term units and permanent homes. A range of different types are required for different needs.

The third factor is *good and reliable support in placement*: support for foster carers, including expert help in dealing with difficult behaviour; help for parents in supporting their child in placement; and above all direct work with children to help them deal with painful transitions and to ensure that they do not feel isolated. Every child should have a trusting relationship with someone outside the home where they are currently living, in part to ensure that problems can be identified and dealt with before they become insuperable. Too often social workers are deterred from developing their skills in direct work with children because of a feeling that there is no time to do it properly and that other aspects of the social work role will always take priority. By re-establishing direct work with children as a central – perhaps the central – part of a social worker's activity, management could do a great deal to improve children's chances of stability and continuity.

Valuing foster carers

During the development phase of the Looking After Children Project many foster carers remarked that the detailed attention to their daily parental actions meant that for the first time they felt their work was fully appreciated. A fact often glossed over in the literature, as we said in Chapter 1, is that 'foster home breakdown' usually means rejection of the looked after child by the foster parents. Anything that increases foster carers' commitment to their task makes it less likely that they will give up when the going gets tough.

Research generally supports the view of the National Foster Care Association that the supply of home-based women prepared to take very difficult children into their homes for no reward is rapidly drying up and that the future lies in professional fostering (NFCA, 1997), although like residential care this may take different forms. In addition foster carers are unanimous that they want to be treated as colleagues, not clients, and to be given a greater degree of autonomy instead of being hedged about with bureaucratic procedures and restrictions.

Paying more for foster care

Related to the last point is the controversial question, does professional foster care, paid at much higher rates, produce greater stability? The research evidence, mostly from the United States and Canada, where 'treatment' foster care has a long history, suggests that it does. One reason is that the payment forms an integral part of the family income and to eject the foster child carries a heavy financial penalty.

A survey of foster carers in Hampshire asked if they thought more people would be willing to care for children if a fee was paid in addition to the maintenance allowance. 86% of the 332 people who responded said it would, but interestingly, when asked about their own motives for caring, the answers they gave were overwhelmingly altruistic. As one respondent said, 'to see a child change from a sullen, angry and sad person to a happy child is worth more than anything money can ever buy' (Gorin, 1997, p.23).

Professional fostering schemes which build in substantial social work support and planned respite for carers, like Pro-Teen, seem to be successful in providing greater stability for the most difficult group, disaffected teenagers. However, an alternative view recently put forward by Kate Wilson and Steph Petrie (1998) is that the 'professionalisation' of foster care and the insistence on distinguishing specific tasks and categories actually works against greater stability.

They point out that traditionally fostering was seen as providing a total, substitute experience in which children would probably have minimal contact with birth relatives, and would form primary attachments with their foster parents, but that gradually the perception of foster care has changed – particularly during the 1970s with Holman's idea of 'inclusive' and 'exclusive' fostering and research which drew attention to importance of links with original family, culminating in the 1980s ideas of 'shared care' and 'partnership'. They argue that the promulgation of inclusive and task-centred models of foster care, reflected in the change of name from 'foster parenting' to 'foster caring', may 'be in danger of minimizing both the attachment needs of many children and young people within the foster placement and the parenting role which is appropriate in many placements' and that alternative models of foster care should be developed – one which stresses these core relationships alongside one which provides for task-centred, time-limited provision.

Advocacy services for children

Advocacy can make an important contribution to maintaining stability, especially at a time of crisis. Just as it is a common feature of incidents of abuse of children in care that children are not listened to, so many of the worst examples of instability are characterised by a failure to hear clearly what children are saying or to take sufficient notice of it. A good advocate can make sure that a child's or young person's voice is heard at the crucial time – whether that be when another move is being considered or when services are needed to support the placement. Social workers are often compromised by their position as employees of the local authority, whereas an independent advocate can represent the child's views and interests without equivocation.

Liean's Story

Liean was a sixteen year old refugee from Ethiopia, who was placed in a private children's home. After a plan for foster care failed to work out, she was told she would have to move to a local authority children's home, despite the fact that she had made friends, was working for GCSEs, and had a disability which meant that a move would have made life extremely difficult for her. Her social worker told Liean that the only alternative would be life on the streets. A school teacher who found her crying gave her details of Childline, who put her in touch with VCC. As a result of their advocacy Liean was allowed to stay where she was until she had completed her GCSEs. She also had a change of social worker.

from Voice for the Child in Care (1998)

Amy's Story

Amy was ten when she came into care and was placed with Kay and Bert. She took to them instantly, felt safe and cared for, and settled down quickly. However the placement was a short-term one and three months later Amy was told that she had been found a new placement closer to school and her mother. She was told that it was costing too much to transport her to her old school.

Amy was worried, had nightmares and became ill. Her father contacted VCC but Social Services would not allow Amy to see an advocate. Eventually she was taken by force to the new placement, and her foster carers were forbidden to contact her. It was only eight months later afer a formal complaint by her father, an application by the local authority for care proceedings and the appointment of a guardian ad litem, that Amy was returned to Kay and Bert.

from Voice for the Child in Care (1998)

Lessons for policy

Placement instability is not only bad for children, it is a very expensive and wasteful use of resources. The point is made by Staff and Fein (1995) in one of the few detailed studies of placement change, that an enormously high proportion of social work time and emotional energy is taken up with change: searching for a suitable placement, preparing children for a move, implementing the move, and dealing with the ensuing results, and most of this effort is concentrated on finding and arranging placements for a relatively small number of children. Even a small reduction in the number of moves would free a great deal of social work time for more productive activities, such as supporting and training foster carers or providing post-adoption counselling and advice.

The variation in numbers of placement moves between authorities (Department of Health, 1998c) suggests that local initiatives to promote stability can be effective, but these need a strong policy lead from the top, supported by elected members, officers and managers. Because, as we have shown, education and placement stability are so interconnected, it is essential that the policy is jointly driven by education and social services.

Clear policies for good practice: a Norwegian example

Slette et al. (1993) provide 'a translation of the ten basic principles that guide Norwegian child welfare practice.' The principles are framed in 'rights' terms and begin:

'Principle 1 – The children's right to continuity and stability must be the primary goal of all attempts at intervention'. The expansion of this principle includes: 'If a child has been moved from a care/treatment placement or has experienced a new placement or an unsuccessful return to the home of origin, and the child again needs placement, the child shall have the right to be returned to the earlier placement should this be deemed (assessed) to be in the best interests of the child. If the child has been returned home to try out the suitability of the home situation, and again must move, then the child must not be moved still another time after that move... Should a crisis occur, the care provider will be given assistance so that a change in caregiver can be avoided... The care provider has the right to expect qualified assistance to avoid the occurrence of unnecessary or unsolvable crises' (translation by Slette et al.)

Leaving care

The point has been made over and over again that young people who have been in care are expected to cope with minimal support at an age when most adolescents can continue to rely on their parents for accommodation, food, financial help and emotional comfort. Leaving care studies have consistently shown that without such support young people lack any kind of security and are at high risk of becoming homeless and destitute (Stein, 1997). Lack of continuity is one of the worst problems for young people moved on at 16, at best to leaving care or independence schemes, and all too often to unsupported lodgings or bedsits. Any benefits to the young person of a stable placement up to that point are likely to be lost, since residential care staff rarely have time to provide continued support and the foster placement may have been officially ended.

If we are serious about creating stability and continuity for looked after children, that commitment must include providing them with a secure base at least up to the age of 18 (and they should be in full time education or training up to that point) and also recognising an obligation to give them any kind of help and support they need if they cannot count on this from their own families, at least until they are 21 or have completed their education. This will usually mean enabling the people or person who cared for them when they were younger to continue to do so at whatever level is wanted (Pro-Teen provides a good model of how this can be done). At present it is entirely a matter of chance whether a young person gets any kind of after care from social services; some local authorities disclaim any duty towards them at the earliest moment they can, while others recognise it as their responsibility to give those they have looked after as children the best possible launch pad into adult life.

Questions that need further research

As we said at the beginning, our most surprising discovery on undertaking this piece of work was that so little high quality research bears directly on the question of stability. We have probably been guilty ourselves of confounding the two separate issues of placement breakdown and placement stability because this happens so often in research reports. Continuity has been addressed by very few researchers, and attracted almost no attention before the Department of Health Working Party on Assessing Outcomes identified it as a major issue for children's services (Parker et al, 1991).

Here are some of the questions to which we could find no answers in the research literature:

- Does the common finding that children placed early enjoy more stability mean that their placements continue to adulthood, or are they at risk of ejection from their foster homes in adolescence? Are the children to whom this happens more or less likely than those placed as teenagers to have multiple placements?

- Why should it ever be necessary for a child to have 10, 20 or 30 different placements?

- Do some local authorities give greater priority to stability and how is this reflected in their policies and management practices?

- What are the outcomes in adult life for children in long-term foster care whose placements do not break down?

- Does children's participation in decision-making lead to greater stability?

- Would better counselling and mental health services for young people reduce the risk of placement change?

- How much would fostering allowances need to be raised to avoid rejection of children with difficult behaviour?

- Does professionalisation of foster care discourage attachment or might it produce greater stability by reducing the emotional demands on carers and young people?

- Is it possible to restore stability to residential care?

- Can the Looking After Children system provide greater continuity for children who have to change placements?

Conclusion

Instability is one of the most serious problems facing the care system today, affecting about half of all children needing long-term care away from home, and almost all those who enter the system as teenagers. It has damaging effects on all aspects of their development, but in particular on their education and their ability to form trusting relationships. For some young people it sets a pattern of dealing with problems by moving on which continues disastrously into their adult life.

Instability of placement is compounded by failure to involve children in decision-making and listen to what they want. Children's own accounts of being looked after too often convey a sense of bewilderment and helplessness, of being pushed around without explanation and for reasons which have more to do with adult agendas than their own. Research into placement breakdown focuses too much on child factors and not enough on the carers and their motivation and the institutional factors that create instability. We can say, though, that even one failure in what is intended to be a long-term placement should set alarm bells ringing, since each move makes the next one more likely, setting in train for some children an accelerating pattern of instability.

We are only at the beginning of any serious efforts to create greater stability. As we have discovered in writing this book, it is a problem which has been seriously neglected both in research and practice. It is too soon to have any confidence about saying what works; most schemes to address the issue are still in their early stages. We know enough to be sure that nothing will change without a strong policy commitment to reduce moves within care to a minimum, both for children who pass through the system and those who need longer term care. Understanding the importance of continuity can do something to mitigate the worst effects of unavoidable placement change, and should be given the highest priority by social workers and managers. Continuity after care as well as during the time when young people are officially 'looked after' is crucial to their functioning and quality of life as adults.

Adoption is a highly controversial subject and will only be relevant to a minority of those looked after by local authorities. Nevertheless on the basis of the evidence we have reviewed we are convinced that it should be considered for a far higher proportion of children who are unlikely to return to their families and welcome the recent government guidance supporting this position. The success rate of adoption in creating stability is already very high, including for children previously considered 'hard to place', and it could be further improved with better provision of preparatory and post-adoption services, which may be needed by any of the people involved at any stage in their lives. We conclude with the words of John Triseliotis, who has made so many important contributions to our understanding of what happens to children when they are separated from their families.

> Over the last half century many studies have contributed to the theory of child development and how children's interests can best be safeguarded and promoted. Knowledge from these studies has influenced child care policy and practice in general, including that of adoption. Much of this knowledge refers to the child's need for continuity of care, security and a sense of belonging to enable him or her to grow into a productive and healthy individual.

> In spite of its many imperfections and despite the increase of divorce and separation, in our kind of society the family or stable households are the place where much needed continuity and relative stability in the life of a child can be provided. When the family into which a child is born cannot provide care, adoption is possibly the best available alternative.

> (Triseliotis et al., 1997)

REFERENCES

Alderson, P., Brill, S., Chalmers, I., Fuller, R., Hinkley-Smith, P., MacDonald, G., Newman, T., Oakley, A., Roberts, H. and Ward, H. (1996) *What Works? Effective social interventions in child welfare*. Barkingside: Barnardos.

Aldgate, J., Bradley, M., and Hawley, D. (1996). 'Respite accommodation: a case study of partnership under the Children Act 1989' in M. Hill and J. Aldgate (eds) *Child Welfare Services: Developments in Law, Policy and Practice*. London: Jessica Kingsley.

Aldgate, J. and Hawley, D. (1986) *Recollections of Disruption: a study of foster care breakdowns*. London: National Foster Care Association.

Atkinson, P. (1990). *The Ethnographic Imagination: textual constructions of reality*. London, Routledge.

Barth, R. and Berry, M. (1988) *Adoption and Disruption: rates, risk and responses*. New York: Aldine de Gruyter.

Beker, J. and Magnuson, D. (eds) (1996) *Residential Education as an Option for At-Risk Youth*. New York: Haworth Press.

Benedict, M., Zuravin, S. and Stallings, R. (1996) 'Adult functioning of children who lived in kin versus non-relative family foster homes', *Child Welfare* **LXXV**(5), 529-549.

Berridge, D. (1996). *Foster Care: a Research Review*. London: HMSO.

Berridge, D. and Brodie, I. (1998) *Children's Homes Revisited*, London: Jessica Kingsley

Berridge, D., Brodie, I. and Beckett, W. (1996) The Health of Children Looked After by Local Authorities, *British Journal of Nursing*, **6**(7) 386-390.

Berridge, D. and Cleaver, H. (1987) *Foster Home Breakdown*. Oxford: Blackwell.

Biehal, N., Clayden, J., Stein, M. and Wade, J. (1995). *Moving On :young people and leaving care schemes.* London: HMSO.

Borland, M. (1991) 'Permanency planning in Lothian Region: the placements', *Adoption and Fostering* **15**(6), 35-40.

Borland, M., Pearson, C., Hill, M., Tisdall, K. and Bloomfield, I. (1998) *Education and Care away from home.* Edinburgh: Scottish Council for Research in Education.

Bourestom, N. (1984). Psychological and physical manifestations of relocation. *Psychiatric Medicine* **2**(1): 57-90.

Bowlby, J. (1991) 'Postcript' in Murray Parkes, C., Stevenson-Hinde, J. and Marris, P. (eds) *Attachment Across the Life Cycle.* London: Routledge.

Broad, B. (1998). *Young People Leaving Care: Life after the Children Act 1989.* London: Jessica Kingsley.

Brown, J. (1998a) *Family and Adolescent Support Services: a Social Services Inspectorate survey of 13 teams in the Northern and Southern Regions by Newcastle Social Service,* London: National Institute for Social Work.

Brown, J. (1998b) 'Family and Adolescent Support Services: new social work crisis, support and assessment services for adolescents and their families.' A discussion paper for the National Institute for Social Work, April 1998.

Bryer, M. (1988) *Planning in Child Care: a guide for team leaders and their teams.* London: British Agencies for Adoption and Fostering.

Bullock, R., Little, M. and Millham, S. (1993) *Going Home: the return of children separated from their families.* Aldershot: Dartmouth.

Butler, S. and Charles, M. (1998) 'Improving the quality of fostering provision: a thematic and dynamic approach' in (ed.) *Exchanging Visions: papers on best practice in Europe for children separated from their birth parents.* London: British Agencies for Adoption and Fostering.

Cairns, B. (1984) 'The Children's Family Trust: a unique approach to substitute family care', *British Journal of Social Work,* **14**, 457-473.

Cairns, B. and Cairns, K. (1989) 'The Family as a Living Group' in A. Brown and R. Clough (eds) *Groups and Grouping: life and work in day and residential centres*. London: Routledge.

Cairns, K. (1999) *Surviving Paedophilia*. Stoke-on-Trent: Trentham Books.

Chamberlain, P., Moreland, S. and Reid, K. (1993) 'Enhanced services and stipends for foster parents: effects on retention rates and outcomes for children', *Child Welfare* **LXXII**(5).

Charles, M., Rashid, S. and Thoburn, J. (1992) 'The placement of black children with permanent new families', *Adoption and Fostering* **16**(3).

Cliffe, D. and Berridge, D. (1991) *Closing Children's Homes*. London: National Children's Bureau.

Colton, M., Drury, C. and Williams, M. (1995) *Children in Need: Family Support under the Children Act 1989*. Aldershot: Avebury.

Colton, M., Hellinckx, W., Ghesquiere, P. and Williams, M. (eds) (1995) *The Art and Science of Child Care: Research, policy and practice in the European Union*. Aldershot: Arena.

Dartington Social Research Unit (no date) *Matching Needs and Services: the audit and planning of provision for children looked after by local authorities*. Totnes: Dartington Social Research Unit.

Department of Health (1998a) 'Adoption- Achieving the Right Balance', Local Authority Circular LAC(98)20.

Department of Health (1998b) *Caring for Children Away from Home: Messages from Research*. Chichester: Wiley.

Department of Health (1998c) 'Children Looked After by Local Authorities Year Ending 31 March 1997, England' (Personal Social Services Local Authority Statistics). London: Stationery Office.

Department of Health and Social Security (1985a) *Social Work Decisions in Child Care*. London: HMSO.

Department of Health and Social Security (1985b) *The Law on Child Care and Family Services*. London: HMSO.

Dolphin Project (1993) *Answering Back: report by young people being looked after on the Children Act 1989*. University of Southampton.

Downes, C. (1992) *Separation Revisited: adolescents in foster family care*. Aldershot: Ashgate.

Dumaret, A.-C. (1988) 'The SOS Children's Villages: school achievement of subjects reared in a permanent foster care', *Early Child Development and Care* **34**, 217-226.

Fahlberg, V. (1994) *A Child's Journey Through Placement*. London: British Agencies for Adoption and Fostering.

Farmer, E. and R. Parker (1991) *Trials and Tribulations: A Study of Children Home on Trial*. London: HMSO.

Fein, E. (1998) 'Secrecy and stigma no longer clouding adoptions', *New York Times*, October 25

Fein, E., Maluccio, A. and Kluger, M. (1990) *No More partings: an examination of long term foster care*. Washington DC: Child Welfare League of America.

Fein, E. and Staff, I. (1993) 'Last best chance: findings from a reunification services program', *Child Welfare* **LXXII**(1), 25-40.

Fenyo, A., Knapp, M. and Baines, B.(1989) 'Foster care breakdown: a study of a special teenage fostering scheme' in Hudson, J. and Galaway, B. (eds) *The State as Parent*. Dordrecht: Kluwer Academic Publishers.

Fischer, C. and Stueve, C. (1977) 'Authentic community: the role of place in modern life' in Fischer, C., Jackson, R. and Stueve, C. (eds) *Networks and Places: Social relations in the urban setting*. New York: Free Press.

Fletcher, B. (1993) *Not Just a Name: the views of young people in foster and residential care*. London: National Consumer Council.

Fletcher-Campbell, F. (1997). *The Education of Children who are Looked-After*. Slough: National Foundation for Educational Research.

Folman, R. (1998) '"I was tooken"', *Adoption Quarterly* **2(2)**, 7-35.

Fraser, M., (ed.) (1997) *Risk and Resilience in Childhood: an ecological perspective*. Washington: National Association of Social Workers.

Fratter, J., Rowe, J., Sapsford, D. and Thoburn, J. (1991) *Permanent Family Placement: a decade of experience*. London: British Agencies for Adoption and Fostering.

Garnett, L. (1992) *Leaving Care and After*. London: National Children's Bureau.

George, V. (1970) *Foster Care: Theory and Practice*. London: Routledge and Kegan Paul.

Gibbs, I. and Sinclair, I. (1998) 'Private and local authority children's homes: a comparison', *Journal of Adolescence*, **21** (5).

Gorin, S. (1997) *Time to Listen? Views and Experiences of Family Placement*, Report No.36, Social Services Research and Information Unit, University of Portsmouth.

Haggerty, R., Sharrod, et al. (1994). *Stress, Risk and Resilience in Children and Adolescents: processes, mechanisms and interventions*. Cambridge: Cambridge University Press.

Hazel, N. (1981). *A Bridge to Independence*. Oxford: Blackwell.

Hazel, N. (1993) 'Theoretical background and evaluation of teenage fostering' in N. Hazel and A. Fenyo (eds.) (1993) *Free to be Myself: the development of teenage fostering*. St.Paul, Minnesota: Human Service Associates

Hazel, N. and Fenyo, A. (eds) (1993) *Free to be Myself: the development of teenage fostering*. St.Paul, Minnesota: Human Service Associates.

Heinicke, C.M. and Westheimer, L. (1965) *Brief Separations*. New York: International Universities Press.

Holloway, J. (1997a) 'Foster and adoptive mothers' assessment of permanent family placements', *Archives of Diseases in Childhood* **76**, 231-235.

Holloway, J. (1997b) 'Outcome in placements for adoption or long-term fostering', *Archives of Diseases in Childhood* **76**, 227-230.

Howe, D. (1995) *Attachment Theory for Social Work Practice*. London: Macmillan.

Hughes, M. (1996) 'Moves of Children in Care', unpublished report for Barnardos Scottish Division.

Hughes, M., Mason, K. and Selman, P. (1998) 'Research for practice: adopting a child with Down's Syndrome: stage 3 of a longitudinal study', *Adoption and Fostering*, **22**(3), 58-9.

Ivaldi, G. (1998) *Children Adopted from Care: an examination of agency adoptions in England*. London: BAAF.

Jackson, S. (1976) The Children Act 1975: parents' rights and children's welfare', *British Journal of Law and Society*, **3**(1).

Jackson, S. (1987) *The Education of Children in Care*, Bristol Papers in Applied Social Studies, No.1, University of Bristol.

Jackson, S. (1989) 'Education of children in care' in B.Kahan (ed.) *Child Care Research, Policy and Practice*. London: Hodder & Stoughton.

Jackson, S. (1994) 'Educating children in residential and foster care', *Oxford Review of Education* **20**(3), 267-279.

Jackson, S. (1998) 'Looking After Children: a new approach or just an exercise in formfilling?', *British Journal of Social Work* **28**(1), 45-56.

Jackson, S. and Kilroe, S. (eds) (1996) *Looking After Children: good parenting, good outcomes: Reader*. London: HMSO.

Jackson, S. and Martin, P. (1998) 'Surviving the care system: education and resilience', *Journal of Adolescence* **21**, 569-583.

Katz, L. (1996) 'Permanency action through concurrent planning', *Adoption and Fostering* **20**(2), 8-13.

Katz, L. and Robinson, C. (1991) '', *Child Welfare* **LXX** Nos 3 and 4.

Kent, R. (1997) *Children's Safeguards Review*. Edinburgh: Scottish Office.

LeProhn, N. and Pecora, P. (1994) *The Casey Foster Parent Study-Research Summary*. Seattle: Casey Family Program.

Levy, A. and Kahan, B. (1991) *The Pindown Experience and the Protection of Children: the Report of the Staffordshire Child Care Inquiry*. Stafford: Staffordshire County Council.

Lewis, J. (1998) 'Building an evidence-based approach to social interventions', *Children and Society* **12**, 136-140.

Link, M. (1996) 'Permanency outcomes in kinship care: a study of children placed in kinship care in Erie County, New York', *Child Welfare* **LXXV**(5), 509-528.

McAuley, C. (1996) *Children in Long-term Foster Care: Emotional and Social Development*. Aldershot: Avebury.

McCollum, A. (1990) *The Trauma of Moving*. Newbury Park: Sage.

Macdonald, G. and Roberts, H. (1995) *What Works in the Early Years?* Barkingside: Barnardos.

Maluccio, A., Fein, E. and Davis, I. (1994) 'Family reunification: research findings, issues and directions',*Child Welfare* **LXXIII**(5), 489-504.

Maluccio, A., Fein, E. and Olmstead, K. (1986) *Permanency Planning for Children: concepts and methods*. London: Tavistock.

Maluccio, A., Pine, B. and Warsh, R. (1994) 'Protecting children by preserving their families', *Children and Youth Services Review*, **16**(5), 295-307.

Marsh, P. and Triseliotis, J. (eds) (1993) *Prevention and Reunification in Child Care*. London: Batsford.

Millham, S., Bullock, R. and Hosie, K. (1986) *Lost in Care*. Aldershot: Gower.

Morgan, P. (1998). *Adoption and the Care of Children*. London: IEA.

National Foster Care Association (1997) *Crisis in Foster Care*. London: NFCA.

Oakley, A. and Roberts, H. (eds) (1996) *Evaluating Social Interventions: a report of two workshops funded by the Economic and Social Research Council*. Barkingside: SSRU/Barnardos.

Palmer, S. (1996) 'Placement stability and inclusive practice in foster care: an empirical study', *Children and Youth Services Review* **18**(7), 589-601.

Parker, R. (1966) *Decision in Child Care – a study of prediction in fostering*. London: George Allen and Unwin.

Parker, R., Ward, H., Jackson, S., Aldgate, J. and Wedge, P. (ed.) (1991) *Looking After Children: assessing outcomes in child care*. London: HMSO.

Quinton, D., Rushton, A., Dance, C. and Mayes, D. (1997) 'Contact between children placed away from home and their birth parents: research issues and evidence', *Clinical Child Psychology and Psychiatry* **2**(3), 393-413.

Robinson, C. (1996) 'Breaks for disabled children' in Stalker, K. (ed.) *Developments in short-Term Care: Breaks and Opportunities*, London: Jessica Kingsley.

Rowe, J., Cain, H., Hundleby, M. and Keane, A. (1984) *Long-Term Foster Care*. London: Batsford.

Rowe, J., Hundleby, M. and Garnett, L. (1989) *Child Care Now: a survey of placement patterns*. London: British Agencies for Adoption and Fostering.

Rowe, J. and Lambert, L. (1973) *Children Who Wait: a study of children needing substitute families*. London: Association of British Adoption Agencies.

Rutter, M. (1997) 'An update on resilience: conceptual considerations and empirical findings' in Meisels, S. and Shonkoff, J. (eds) *Handbook of Early Childhood Intervention*. New York: Cambridge University Press.

Rutter, M. and the English and Romanian Adoptees Study Team (1998) 'Developmental catch-up and deficit following adoption after severe global early privation', *Journal of Child Psychology and Psychiatry* **39**(4), 465-476.

Sanders, R., Jackson, S. and Thomas, N. (1996) 'The balance of prevention, investigation and treatment in the management of child protection services', *Child Abuse & Neglect* **20**(10), 899-906.

Scannapieco, M. (1999) 'Kinship care in the public child welfare system: a systematic review of the research' in Hegar, R. L. and Scannapieco, M. (eds) *Kinship Foster Care: policy, practice and research*. New York: Oxford University Press.

Secretary of State for Health (Rt.Hon. Frank Dobson) (1998) *Modernising Social Services: Promoting independence, Improving protection, Raising standards*, Cm 41169, London: Stationery Office.

Sellick, C. and Thoburn, J. (1996) *What Works in Family Placement?* Barkingside, Barnardos.

Shaw, C. (1998) *Remember My Messages*. London: Who Cares? Trust.

Sinclair, R. , Garnett, L. and Berridge, D. (1995) *Social Work and Assessment with Adolescents*. London: National Children's Bureau.

Skinner, A. (1992) *Another Kind of Home: a review of residential child care*. Edinburgh: Social Work Services Inspectorate for Scotland.

Slette, S., Hagen, G. and Maier, H. (1993) 'Permanency planning principles in the Norwegian child welfare system and their application to practice', *Child Welfare* **LXX11**(1), 77-88.

Social Work Services Inspectorate for Scotland (1996) *A Secure Remedy: A review of the role, availability and quality of secure accommodation for children in Scotland*. Edinburgh: HMSO.

Staff, I. and Fein, E. (1995) 'Stability and change: initial findings in a study of treatment foster care placements', *Children and Youth Services Review* **17** (3), 379-389.

Stein, M. (1997) *What Works in Leaving Care?* Barkingside, Barnardos.

Stein, T., Gambrill, E. and Wiltse, K. (1978) *Children in Foster Homes: Achieving Continuity of Care*. New York: Praeger.

Tam, T. and Ho, M. (1996) 'Factors influencing the prospect of children returning to their parents from out-of-home care', *Child Welfare* **LXXV**(3), 253-268.

Thoburn, J. (1990) *Success and Failure in Permanent Family Placement*. Aldershot: Avebury.

Thoburn, J., Murdoch, A. and O'Brien, A. (1986) *Permanence in Child Care*. Oxford: Blackwell.

Thoburn, J. and Rowe, J. (1988) 'A snapshot of permanent family placement', *Adoption and Fostering* **12**(3), 29-34.

Thomas, N. and Beckett, C. (1994) 'Are children still waiting? New developments and the impact of the Children Act 1989', *Adoption and Fostering* **18**(1), 8-16.

Thomas, N. and O'Kane, C. (1998) *Children and Decision Making: a summary report*. University of Wales Swansea: International Centre for Childhood Studies.

Thomas, N. and O'Kane, C. (forthcoming) 'Children's participation in reviews and planning meetings when they are 'looked after' in middle childhood', *Child and Family Social Work* **4**.

Tizard, B. (1977) *Adoption: a Second Chance*. London: Open Books.

Trasler, G. (1960) *In Place of Parents: a study of foster care*. London: Routledge and Kegan Paul.

Triseliotis, J. , Borland, M., Hill, M. and Lambert L. (1995) *Teenagers and Social Work Services*. London: HMSO.

Triseliotis, J. and Russell, J. (1984) *Hard to Place – The outcome of adoption and residential care*. Aldershot: Gower.

Triseliotis, J., Sellick, C. and Short, R. (1995) *Foster Care: theory and practice*. London: Batsford.

Triseliotis, J., Shireman, J. and Hundleby, M. (1997). *Adoption: theory, policy and practice*. London: Cassell.

Utting, Sir W. (1991) *Children in the Public Care: a Review of Residential Child Care*. London: Department of Health/HMSO.

Utting, Sir W. (1997) *People Like Us: the report of the review of the safeguards for children living away from home*. London: Stationery Office.

Voice for the Child in Care (1998) *Shout to be Heard: Stories from Young People in Care about getting heard and using advocates*. London: Voice for the Child in Care.

Walby, C. (1998) *Review of Children's Services Plans in Wales*. Cardiff: Welsh Office.

Ward, H. (ed.) (1995) *Looking After Children: research into practice*. London: HMSO.

Weiner, A. and Weiner, E. (1990) *Expanding the Options in Child Placement: Israel's dependent children in care from infancy to adulthood*. New York: University Press of America.

Whitaker, D., Archer, L. and Hicks, L. (1998) *Working in Children's Homes: Challenges and Complexities*. Chichester: Wiley.

Wilson, K. and Petrie, S. (1998) 'No place like home: lessons learned and lessons forgotten – the Children Act 1948', *Child and Family Social Work* 3(3), 183-188.

Yelloly, M. (1979) 'Independent Evaluation of 25 Placements'. Maidstone: Kent County Council Social Services Department.